The Patrick Kavanagh Poetry Award Winners,
1971–2003

O dance with Kitty Stobling I outrageously
Cried out-of-sense to them ...

Patrick Kavanagh, 'Come Dance with Kitty Stobling'

The Patrick Kavanagh
Poetry Award Winners,
1971–2003

Edited by Antoinette Quinn

The Lilliput Press Dublin
in association with **The Patrick Kavanagh Society**

In memory of Magdalene Quinn

First published 2004 by
THE LILLIPUT PRESS
62–63 Sitric Road, Arbour Hill,
Dublin 7, Ireland
www.lilliputpress.ie

The cover image of *The Long Woman's Dream* by Gerard Dillon
is reproduced by kind permission of the painter's nephew, Gerard Dillon.

A CIP record for this title is available from
The British Library.

ISBN 1 84351 045 6

The Lilliput Press receives financial assistance from
An Chomhairle Ealaíon / The Arts Council of Ireland.

Printed by ColourBooks, Baldoyle, Dublin

CONTENTS

Acknowledgments

The Patrick Kavanagh Society and The Lilliput Press thank the following poets, poets' executors and publishers for their kind permission to print the poems in this anthology:

Nuala Archer for 'love to my friends, family, sweethearts and self in ireland' and 'Eight Untitled Suaimhneach Songs'.

Pat Boran and The Dedalus Press, Dublin, for 'House' from *The Unwound Clock* (1990); 'Children' from *Familiar Things* (1993); 'A Natural History of Armed Conflict', 'Still Life with Carrots' and 'Neighbours' from *As the Hand, the Glove* (2001).

Rory Brennan and The Dolmen Press, Dublin, for 'This Knotted Cord' and 'Security' from *The Sea on Fire* (1979); also The Dedalus Press for 'The Oil Lamp', 'The Threshing Circles and 'The Other Islands' from *The Walking Wounded* (1985); also Salmon Poetry, Clare, for 'The Paper Kisses', 'The Wind Messages' and 'Elsewhere and Clonmacnoise' from *The Old in Rapallo* (1996).

Seán Clarkin for 'N.B. pages 6 & 7', 'After Mass, Curracloe', 'Notes from a Winter's Day', 'Inniskeen, November Evening' and 'Autumn Blues'; also The Gallery Press, Loughcrew, Oldcastle, Co. Meath, for 'September Song' from *Without Frenzy* (1974); also The Dedalus Press for 'New Ross Poem' from *At the year's turning or volge l'anno* (1998).

Harry Clifton and The Gallery Press for 'Ireland' from *Comparative Lives* (1982); 'At the Grave of Silone' and 'The River' from *Night Train through the Brenner* (1994).

Michael Coady and The Gallery Press for 'The Bayonet' from *Two for a Woman, Three for a Man* (1980); 'Assembling the Parts' from *Oven Lane* (1987); 'The Club' from *All Souls* (1997); 'Adhlacadh an Dreoilín' and 'Normal Singing' from *One Another* (2003).

Roz Cowman for 'The Robber Bride', 'Meanings', 'Longonot Crater Kenya 1968', 'The Kitchen Window', 'Quadrille at the Duchess of Richmond's Ball'; also Salmon Poetry for 'The Goose Herd' and 'Annunciation' from *The Goose Herd* (1989).

Celia de Fréine for 'Cherubin, My Eye', 'Heavy Weather', 'Let Him Skip Hence', 'In the Land of Wince and Whinny' and 'Just Dessert in Gran Canaria'.

Greg Delanty and Carcanet Press, Manchester, for 'Striped Ink' from *The Hellbox* (1998); 'The Marriage Stitch', 'International Call' and 'Behold the Brahmany Kite' from *The Blind Stitch* (2001); and 'The Alien' from *The Ship of Birth* (2003).

Paul Durcan and Anna Livia Press, Dublin, for 'Nessa' and 'November 30, 1967' from *O Westport in the Light of Asia Minor* (1975); also The Harvill Press, London, for 'Waterloo Road' from *Greetings to Our Friends in Brazil* (1999).

John Ennis and The Gallery Press for 'Sgarúint na gCompánach' from *Night on Hibernia* (1976); and 'James' from *Dolmen Hill* (1977); also The Dedalus Press for 'Against the Wood' from *In a Green Shade* (1991); 'Illumination' and 'Vedic' from *Down in the Deeper Helicon* (1994).

Carmel Fitzsimons for 'Bombers', 'Bonnard', 'Clothes', 'Love Lets You Go;

For My Father', 'A Lullaby for Ellie' and 'I wish …'.

Anthony Glavin for 'Nine Poems from a Work-in-Progress'; also The Gallery Press for 'Born Losers' from *The Wrong Side of the Alps* (1989).

Austin Greene and Salmon Poetry for 'Silence and the Blue Night', 'Letting Go' and 'Terrorist's Wife' from *Silence and the Blue Night* (1993) by Angela Greene.

Ann Leahy for 'Mince Customer', 'Sorcerer', 'Cold Storage' 'A House Divided' and 'A Good Rogeting'.

Alice Lyons for 'Unfinished Painting', 'Paintings of Martyrs Speak', 'The Polish Language' and 'Thank God It's Dry'.

Michael McCarthy and Bradshaw Books, Cork, for 'Birds' Nests', 'Sam Gosling's Corner', 'The Gift', 'In Memoriam' and 'After the Wedding' from *Birds' Nests and Other Poems* (2003).

Thomas McCarthy for 'Nathaniel Murphy Considers *The Edinburgh Review*, 1811', 'Mr Nathaniel Murphy in His Sister's Bedroom, 1798' and 'Lady Nora Wingfield, Mrs Nat Hutchins, Lady Keane'; also The Dolmen Press for 'Daedalus, the Maker' from *The First Convention* (1978); also Anvil Press Poetry, London, for 'Question Time' from *The Non-Aligned Storyteller* (1984).

Manus McManus for 'Story', 'Waking in Pennsylvania, Near the Irish Sea', 'The Remote Loves of Men', 'Houses of Cape May', 'At Rickett's Glen' and 'It Is Not Often that I Write'.

Aidan Mathews for 'At the Junction', 'Imperial War Museum', 'Decency', 'After Omagh'; also The Dolmen Press for 'Returning to Kilcoole' from *Windfalls* (1977).

Áine Miller and Salmon Poetry for 'Seventeen' from *Goldfish in a Baby Bath* (1994); 'In His Eye', 'Man-Child', 'Adam' and 'Begotten' from *Touchwood* (2000).

Sinéad Morrissey for 'The Cave Hill in February', 'Migraine', 'Driving Alone on a Snowy Evening', 'Genetics' and 'From *The State of the Prisons: A History of John Howard, Prison Reformer, 1726–1790*'.

Eiléan Ní Chuilleanáin for 'In the Hills' and 'The Married Women'; also The Gallery Press for 'Bessboro', 'Agnes Bernelle', 'In Her Other House', 'In Her Other Ireland' and 'Inheriting the Books' from *The Girl Who Married the Reindeer* (2001).

Eibhlín Nic Eochaidh for 'On Learning to Read', 'Her Blue Cardigan', 'What She Remembers Now', 'How to Kill a Living Thing' and 'Holding the Space'.

Conor O'Callaghan and The Gallery Press for 'The Ocean' from *The History of Rain* (1993); 'Green Baize Couplets' and 'The Oral Tradition' from *Seatown* (1999); 'Gloves' and 'The Count' from a forthcoming publication.

Sheila O'Hagan for 'September the Fourth', 'Elegy for Mark' and 'Angel Preening'; also Salmon Poetry for 'Mozart's Kitchen' from *The Peacock's Eye* (1992); 'The Return of Odysseus to Ithaca' and 'The Troubled House' from *The Troubled House* (1995); also Bradshaw Books for 'Mirage' from *Poems for the Millennium* (2000).

Tom O'Malley and Beaver Row Press, Dublin, for 'Grief' from *By Lough Mask* (1985); also Salmon Poetry for 'Travelling

Shop', 'The Mallard', 'Time-Share', 'Spring Cleaning', 'Roots and Instincts' and 'Garden Fire' from *Journey Backward* (1998).

Padraig Rooney for 'His Winter Laboratory', 'The Whirligig Dream', 'Proust's Day', 'Pool' and 'The Disappearing Act'.

Peter Sirr and The Gallery Press for 'The King in the Forest' from *Marginal Zones* (1984); 'Vigils' from *Talk, Talk* (1987); ' "Of the thousand ways to touch you" ' from *Ways of Falling* (1991); 'Cures' from *The Ledger of Fruitful Exchange* (1995); and 'Peter Street' from *Bring Everything* (2000).

Bill Tinley for 'Epithalamium', 'First Thoughts on the Death of Joseph Brodsky', 'Aubade, Winter', 'Gethsemane Revisited' and 'Tennis Courts in Snow'; also New Island Books, Dublin, for 'Danaë' from *Grace* (2001).

William Wall and The Collins Press, Cork, for '*from* The Wake in the House' and 'Radiance' from *Mathematics and Other Poems* (1997); also The Dedalus Press for 'The Stairs Unlit', 'Alfred Russell Wallace in the Molluccas' and 'The Wasps' Nest' from *Fahrenheit Says Nothing To Me* (2004).

Joseph Woods for 'An Occasional House of Her Father's', 'Landship', 'Interview', 'A Carvery Lunch in Louth' and 'Plastic Butterflies'.

Some of the poems reprinted here first appeared in *Barrow Street*, *Cuirt*, *The Irish Times*, *Litspeak Dresden*, *Poetry Ireland Review*, *The SHOp*, *The Sunday Tribune*. 'Gethsemane Revisited' by Bill Tinley was first published by *Poetry* (Chicago).

Every effort has been made to trace copyright holders and The Lilliput Press would be glad to be informed of any oversight.

The Patrick Kavanagh Society gratefully acknowledges the financial assistance of Monaghan County Council, County Monaghan VEC and Louth County Council in the publication of this anthology. Thanks are due to Declan Nelson, Manager, Monaghan County Council; Larry McCluskey, Chief Executive Officer of County Monaghan VEC; and Brian Harten, Arts Officer, Louth County Council, who arranged the donations. Special thanks are due to Larry McCluskey, the overall organizer of this sponsorship.

The Society also wishes to thank those who helped with the anthology in a variety of ways: Fiona Ahern; Brendan Barrington; Kate Bateman; Padraig Clerkin, Monaghan County Museum; Dympna Condra, County Monaghan Tourism Officer; Brian Crowley; Dr Patrick Duffy; the Greene family, Drogheda; Fern Heasty; Maurice Henry; Rita Henry; Catherine Marshall and Marguerite O'Molloy of IMMA; Maeve McCluskey; Barry O'Brien and the Royal College of Surgeons; Joseph Woods, Director of Poetry Ireland. The Society is especially grateful to Graham Thew, who designed this book, and to Marsha Swan for her meticulous attention to detail in copy-editing the text.

Introduction

Dancing with Kitty Stobling, an anthology by the thirty-two winners of the Patrick Kavanagh Poetry Award, is presented as a tribute to Patrick Kavanagh on the centenary of his birth. The title is based on that of his finest collection, *Come Dance with Kitty Stobling*, the Spring Choice of the London-based Poetry Society in 1960.

Dancing with Kitty Stobling does not claim to offer a comprehensive cross-section of the best Irish poetry since Kavanagh's death. The fact that from the outset the award was restricted to an unpublished or recently published first collection meant that it excluded a talented group of relatively young poets who had published one or more individual collections in the 1960s, among them Eavan Boland, Seamus Heaney, Brendan Kennelly, John Montague, Michael Longley, Derek Mahon and James Simmons. Moreover, some poets chose not to compete and some runners-up found a publisher for their collection immediately rather than compete again. In most instances, however, the judges' decision has been endorsed by publishers, literary critics and the verdict of adjudicators in later competitions. If the names of judges and runners-up as well as those of winners were to be taken into account, then the award's significant place in Irish poetry since Kavanagh's death would be clearer. On hearsay evidence it would appear that almost every Irish poet writing today has been involved in the award in one way or another at some time in its history.

What *Dancing with Kitty Stobling* attests to is the thematic variety and technical assurance of the poetry being produced by some of the best Irish writers. It also suggests the remarkable amount of verse being produced in Ireland. Behind every poet published here are fifty to three hundred others who failed to win the award or be a runner-up in any given year; this gives an idea of the scale of poetic activity in Ireland over the past thirty years.

The Patrick Kavanagh Poetry Award, now in its thirty-third year, is Ireland's longest-running annual award for a first collection of poems. It was established just four years after the poet's death by the newly formed Patrick Kavanagh Society based in Co. Monaghan. The first members of the Society can hardly have foreseen that the award would continue into the next millennium and make such a significant contribution to Irish literary history.

Largely on the initiative of the dramatist Eugene McCabe, the Patrick Kavanagh Society was founded at a public meeting in Castleblayney Town Hall on 14 November 1970. For the first three years most meetings took place there; after 1973 the Society moved its base to the poet's native village, Inniskeen. From the outset, membership was largely drawn from Co. Monaghan, one distinguished exception being the Co. Louth poet Jim Craven. The first committee comprised Chairman Eugene McCabe (Clones), Vice-Chairman James Deery (Inniskeen), Secretary Martin Hanratty (Castleblayney), Hon. Treasurer Mackey Rooney (Monaghan), Assistant Treasurer Peter Murphy (Inniskeen), along with members Gerald Gillanders, John and Tommy McArdle (all from Castleblayney), Gene Carroll, John and Tom Lennon, Tom and Magdalene Quinn, May Treacy (all from Inniskeen), and Jim Craven (Dundalk). The new Society's two main concerns were the annual commemoration of Patrick Kavanagh's death and the establishment of a literary award in his honour.

A first commemoration ceremony held on 29 November 1970 set the pattern for subsequent years. The commemoration would always take place on the afternoon of the last Sunday in November and consist of the laying of a wreath on Patrick Kavanagh's grave in Inniskeen churchyard, often by a member of the poet's family, followed by a reading of a selection of Kavanagh's poetry and a concert or other entertainment.

The Patrick Kavanagh Poetry Award was inaugurated by the Society in 1971 after much debate as to whether it should be restricted to Co. Monaghan poets or to poets under twenty or be extended to writers of all ages and genres, and whether it should reward achievement or promise. A sub-committee, chaired by Sir Tyrone Guthrie, was set up to explore the issue, but he died in November 1971, shortly before the presentation of the first award.

There were sixty-one entrants for this first award of £100, which was won by Seán Clarkin for an unpublished collection of poems. He was over twenty and a native of Co. Wexford, so the advocates of an all-Ireland award for a new poetry collection by a poet of any age had succeeded in establishing a precedent. Although the debate continued for a couple of years, the future course of the award was already determined. When Seán Clarkin was invited to read his poems in Inniskeen on Commemoration Sunday 1971, another tradition was invented. The poetry award and the anniversary ceremony would thereafter be linked.

Discussions as to its nature and purpose in 1972 prevented any award being made. After this the Patrick Kavanagh Poetry Award became an annual event. In its early years it was restricted to an unpublished collection of more than twenty poems or a collection published the previous year. However, since the Society considered that the identity of the competitors should be concealed from the judges, each entry being assigned a number rather than a name, the possibility of submitting an already published collection soon had to be abandoned. The emphasis on anonymity was gradually extended to the judges as well; at one meeting the Society chairman who knew the judges' names thought it improper to divulge them even to his own committee. This culture of secrecy continued until quite recently and very few judges are named in the Society's records.

Today the Patrick Kavanagh Poetry Award is open to poets born on the island of Ireland or of Irish nationality or long-term residents in Ireland who have not previously published a collection. In addition to the winner there are two named runners-up. Unfortunately, since the Society's records are incomplete, it is not possible to list the runners-up and only the winners are represented in the present volume.

Over the years membership of the Society has changed as members resigned or died and new members joined. Eugene McCabe resigned as chairman in 1974, although he continued his involvement with the Society for several years. When Ben Kiely took over from him the position became largely honorary and meetings were conducted by the Vice-Chairman, James Deery, who was succeeded by Tom Quinn. In 1976 the Society decided to opt for an honorary president and an active chairman. Nevertheless, the first president, Senator Eoin Ryan, who remained in office until his death in 2001, took a lively interest in the Society's affairs, often acting in an advisory capacity or helping to arrange sponsorship for the poetry award. Tom Quinn became chairman from 1976 until he died in 1983, when he was succeeded by the present incumbent, Peter Murphy. In the Society's early years John and Tommy McArdle were frequently called upon to advise on the appointment of judges for the poetry award or to arrange entertainment for Commemoration Sunday.

Other members, besides those already mentioned, who for many years played a key role in the Society and in the continuance of its poetry award, include Ned Coleman, Mrs Cumiskey, Bernard Cunningham, Celia Cunningham, Mrs Hanratty, Larry McCluskey, Gerry Murphy, Clinton and Emily O'Rourke and Sandra Rooney. At present the Society is administered by a committee consisting of Peter Murphy (Chairman), Rosaleen Kearney and Daig Quinn (Joint Secretaries), and members Art and Helen Agnew, Sr Una

Agnew, Gene Carroll, Seamus Cassidy, Larry McDermott and Thomas Ruddy.

In 1974 the Patrick Kavanagh Poetry Award gained its first sponsor, Lough Egish Creamery, which was followed by the Northern Standard; Irish Distillers; P.J. Carroll; Stokes, Kennedy, Crowley; New Ireland Assurance; and Portobello College. There were several anxious years in the 1990s when corporate sponsorship was difficult to come by and in 1994 it was decided to charge competitors an entry fee of £10 and reduce the number of judges from three to two in an attempt to make ends meet. In recent years the prize money has been generously donated by the Inniskeen firm, Primepack.

From the late 1980s until her death in 2001 the poetry award was administered almost single-handedly by the secretary Magdalene Quinn, who persisted in maintaining it as an annual event despite the Society's often precarious financial state. The survival of the award to the present day is largely due to her unflagging zeal and determination. *Dancing with Kitty Stobling* is dedicated to her memory and the collection includes an elegy, 'November Evening, Inniskeen', written for her by Seán Clarkin, who has attended almost every Commemoration Sunday since 1971.

Today the deconsecrated Catholic church, situated in the graveyard where Patrick Kavanagh and his wife, Katherine, are buried, is a Patrick Kavanagh Rural and Literary Resource Centre administered by the Inniskeen Enterprise Development Group and managed by the friendly and knowledgable Rosaleen Kearney. It has become an essential port of call for visitors to Kavanagh Country. In addition to imparting a wealth of information about Kavanagh, the Centre offers tours guided by Gene Carroll, well known for his dramatic renderings of the poet's works in an authentic Inniskeen accent. The wreath-laying ceremony is now the culmination of an annual Patrick Kavanagh Weekend held in the Centre. Patrick Kavanagh may have 'inclined / To lose … faith in Ballyrush and Gortin', but his native village has kept faith with him.

Over the past thirty-three years the Patrick Kavanagh Poetry Award has become part of the fabric of Irish literary history. In its early years it was one of the very few awards specifically designed for Irish poets and elicited an overwhelming response: there were more than three hundred entries in 1974. For many poets, winning the award outright or being a runner-up was the first significant step in their literary career. Such is the prestige of the award that it continues to attract large numbers of competitors: in 2003 there were nearly two hundred entries.

Dancing with Kitty Stobling is not intended to be the swan-song of the Patrick Kavanagh Poetry Award. This rich and diverse collection offers the poetry-lover an opportunity to reread some old favourites, to encounter new or previously uncollected poems by well-known names, and to discover fresh, new talent, especially among the contributions of recent winners. All the poems have been chosen by the poets themselves rather than reflecting the taste or thematic bias of the anthologist. It is to be assumed that contributors have chosen to be represented by pieces they particularly like, giving readers a rare insight into each poet's own preferences.

Whereas some anthologies adopt a hierarchical approach, assigning a number of pages to contributors dependant on their perceived literary status, here all poets were invited to present five pages and include a poem from the award-winning collection. Not all contributors complied, though in most cases the first poem in each poet's section is from this first collection. Original work was neither solicited nor expected, yet some established poets, among them Roz Cowman, Anthony Glavin, Aidan Mathews, Thomas McCarthy, Sinéad Morrissey and Eiléan Ní Chuilleanáin, have generously given uncollected or even unpublished work.

Listing the winners chronologically reveals that in the first half of the award's history, up to 1987, only two were women – Eiléan Ní Chuilleanáin and Roz Cowman – whereas from then on the gender balance has tipped the other way and nine of the remaining sixteen winners are female. A possible explanation, since from quite early on all entries were anonymous, is that this arose from a then prevalent bias in Ireland against the propriety of writing poems on domestic or feminine themes that Eavan Boland expounds so eloquently in her 1989 pamphlet, *A Kind of Scar: The Woman Poet in a National Tradition* (Attic Press, Dublin). Such a bias might have affected the judges' verdict or it might have silenced or intimidated some potential women poets.

A geographical profile of award-winners shows that most grew up in the cities of Dublin or Cork or live there now, with the majority based in Dublin. Yet becoming an Irish poet is not an urban phenomenon. Galway and Limerick have produced no winners to date and, Dublin and Cork apart, winners are drawn from ten counties. Despite the original intention to restrict the competitors to Co. Monaghan, so far Padraig Rooney has been the only winner from there. Three winners – Sinéad Morrissey, Conor O'Callaghan and Celia de Fréine – come from Northern Ireland and three – Nuala Archer, Carmel Fitzsimons and Alice Lyons – are offspring of the Irish diaspora.

Unlike the largely self-taught Patrick Kavanagh, most of the award-winners are university graduates and three of the more recent (Joseph Woods, Áine Miller and Eibhlín Nic Eochaidh) have a master's degree in creative writing. While poetry could hardly be classified as one of the more lucrative professions, it is a good time to be a poet in Ireland. In Kavanagh's lifetime bursaries or awards for Irish poets were few and readings and writers-in-residence schemes were very rare. Today literary prizes abound and the proliferation of readings, workshops conducted by poets, writers-in-residence and writers-in-schools schemes provide paid opportunities for poets to meet their public and market their wares. For those elected, membership of Aosdána ensures a regular stipend.

The biographies of the award-winners demonstrate that Ireland is culturally vibrant and that Irish society is willing to create job opportunities for its poets. Although most poets in the anthology have lived and worked elsewhere in Europe, or in Asia, Africa or America for several years, only four of those born in Ireland have chosen to live abroad: Harry Clifton, Greg Delanty, Michael McCarthy and Padraig Rooney.

Patrick Kavanagh once sardonically remarked that the standing army of Irish poets rarely falls below ten thousand. What would he make of today's prolific poetic industry? Would he approve of the award named after him?

Characteristically, Kavanagh would be caustic about some contemporary Irish bards. Yet, although he was harshly dismissive of much of the verse being produced in Ireland in his time, he was also very well disposed towards young poets whose work had 'merit'. Anthony Cronin experienced this in 1950 when Kavanagh complimented him on his poem 'For the Father' in the May issue of *Envoy*, and thereafter befriended him. Among those beginners whose poetry he praised in the last year of his life was one of the earliest winners of the Patrick Kavanagh Poetry Award, Paul Durcan.

In general, Kavanagh approved of awards and patronage, any form of sponsorship that would set the poet free to write. He competed enthusiastically for the few awards available in his day. We know that at age twenty-four and twenty-five he was fifteen times a runner-up for the prize of one guinea in the *Irish Weekly Independent's* weekly poetry competition. The only literary prize Kavanagh ever won was the first AE Memorial Award of £100 in 1940. On this occasion the author of *Ploughman and Other Poems* and *The Green Fool* faced stiff competition from Brian O'Nolan, who had just published his brilliant novel, *At Swim-Two-Birds*.

Sixteen years were to pass before Kavanagh became eligible for another award. The annual Guinness Poetry Award, which operated between 1956 and 1961, was unlike most other literary prizes in that poets did not compete directly. Organizers collected the best of the poems published in British and Irish magazines in a given year and submitted them to the three appointed judges. Kavanagh, who had not succeeded in winning a Guinness award during the first two years, was appointed a judge in the third. Probably on the principle, 'If you can't beat them, judge them,' he happily undertook the arduous task for the three remaining years of the award, glad of the generous honorarium and the perk of travel to and from London, where he was put up in the smart Brown's Hotel.

Finally, months before Kavanagh's death in 1967 when he was too ill to write and his new wife, Katherine, had to go out to work to support them both, his publisher, Tim O'Keeffe of MacGibbon and Kee, petitioned the Irish and British Arts Councils on the ailing poet's behalf. To its lasting shame, the Irish Arts Council procrastinated and it was the British Arts Council that came to Kavanagh's rescue, awarding him a poetry bursary of £1200, thereby ensuring that he died, as he had seldom lived, in credit with his bank.

'O dance with Kitty Stobling', Patrick Kavanagh exhorted his audience in the title poem of *Come Dance with Kitty Stobling*. There he envisaged his 'rhyme/Cavorting on mile-high stilts' across the 'colourful country' to the amazement and terror of earthbound onlookers. Kitty Stobling was his outrageous, zany, carefree muse, leading him on to scorn rationality and respectability and indulge his high spirits in high jinks.

In *Dancing with Kitty Stobling*, the thirty-two winners of the poetry award instituted in Patrick Kavanagh's honour respond to his challenge, joyfully celebrating in verse the centenary of his birth.

1971

Seán Clarkin was born in New Ross, Co. Wexford, in 1941 and lived there until he was eighteen. He studied at the Gregorian University in Rome, at University College Cork and at Trinity College Dublin. He has spent many years managing a bookshop in Wexford and teaching with Co. Wexford VEC, mostly in Bridgetown Vocational College. He is also involved in Poetry Ireland's 'Writers in Schools' programme.

He first became interested in poetry in Rome in the sixties. It was while recovering from a near-fatal accident during his student years at Cork university that he responded to the Patrick Kavanagh Society's advertisement of its first award. Since then he has been a regular attender at the Kavanagh annual commemoration in Inniskeen.

'September Song' is from *Without Frenzy* (The Gallery Press 1974), based on his award-winning collection. 'New Ross Poem' was included in *At the year's turning or volge l 'anno*, (The Dedalus Press 1998). The other poems here are previously unpublished. He is currently working on a new poetry collection and a novel.

Seán Clarkin lives in Curracloe, Co. Wexford. He is married to Nora and they have two grown-up children, Anne and Owen.

September Song

Keep the steeple behind you
& the church
hidden below those sloping fields.

Keep too
an eye to the wind and smile:

the brazen rowan
still smiles
at the berried sun

ignoring
the rook's voice
the jaundiced ash
the neighbour who died
at the yellow door.

There are tears in the eyes
Of the sunflower in September.

New Ross Poem

To view the corner of a graveyard
day after day.
To see the woman coming to the door
randomly.
Wrinkled smoker. Observer observed.

To see a strip of tarmac
down which coffins come
carefully.

To listen to the blackbird
fight off the magpie
day after rainsoaked day
till we wear out this tedious time.

Meanwhile, the leaves turn
their silver lining
in the gentle breeze
and the man preparing the coffins comes to tea.

This corner of a field
will wear out our wretched curiosity.

N.B. pages 6 & 7

Half and half ...
    not a mathematical precision
    but a generous
    distribution
      of itself
        into
          2 blobs
      of deadfly.

Its death was a casual happening: a personal tragedy.
No need to read between the lines.

After Mass, Curracloe

We manoeuvre down the aisle
like sheep to a drinking pen,
begin to exchange greetings halfway
down. The mystery is gone out of this place.

Outside, released from the gloom
cars start up; their lights
turning the graveyard into some crazy disco
    As the red brake-lights mingling
    with the yellow indicators
    and the strong plain lights
    dance across the few yards of gravel
to bounce and flicker among the coloured marble
and the plainness of limestone.

The stones are frozen dancers.
Somebody turned off the music.
Turn off the lights.
These are the settled community.

Notes from a Winter's Day

The stars are out tonight,
   winking the old wink
and the trees are saying something
that may be the same as the chimney's whisper.

You'd know – I'm new here.

And over the door – the big imposing
front door,
below my darkening window, the 'Plough':
an image lost from the fields
but lying now in any corner of the old sky
that we pollute willy-nilly like we do an old ditch.

I write to tell you
Your cat has delivered up
The room to a new guest.

Late twilight
closes the lake

like the lid a tired eye.

Inniskeen, November Evening

The carpets are outside the house
now.
Leaf pattern after leaf pattern.
Cotton-easter vulgar in speckled red.

The chestnut, guarding the gate,
has resigned.
The hydrangea by the wall
has autumn sickness

A delicate
Filigreed chair
Islanded on the lawn
Is tomb furniture
Stark in its whiteness.

The shadow in an upstairs window –
a lone Penates;*
its back to everything that might be happening
or has happened:

Your coffin in the lit hearse for example,
the old concrete fence at the gate;
A moon *ghosting* the silence in the new absence;
You and Tom leaving for the weddings.
The postman delivering poem-burdens.
One or two unmemorable journeys

A poet snooping around the house.

I do not find your grave.
Drumlin follows drumlin. A houseless hill. Black hills too.

I find silence and autumn.
Autumn is a damp wreath.

*Penates – Roman household gods

Autumn Blues

Peculiar, if exact, use of words:

'New delivery of old furniture – Friday 23rd'
Adjectives playing old tricks in a window among dust.

Blackwater on a bright autumn day. A place
Looking forward, if only to the 23rd.
Appreciating old stuff.

Today, the lights go out.
They don't come back on ...

Maybe never,
though I can't tell.

In a local store
I pile the counter with cans of this and that:
beans of course and tomato sauce ...
and peas (extra 20% free).
Soups (always chicken and Campbells) ...
tuna, spam.
Other tins.
Wine and water (2 by 5 litres)
& batteries, many and expensive.

What is happening?
you may well ask.
The tabloid heading **'Sellafield a target'** might
be sensational or true. The righteous are bombing Afghanistan.
As I say, the lights go out. The till stops winking.

I have no cash. 'We can't use your credit card' ... herself
And the machine. The Royal 'We'.
And the lights stay out
And the machine.

Outside in the sunlight, the village centre ticks over
And a bearded character leans on the parapet

of the bridge as he should do.
At the back a man, a young man, struggles
with a generator.
The plastic bags containing the tins reach
Their arms every which way.

Not to desert them, I carry
my copy of a magazine with the headline: 'Why
They Hate America' next door to the pub. Darkness
follows me. No chance of a hot Irish whiskey.

I am
coming down with flu, sure as god.

The boy
is only settling into the day. The kettle is cold and
empty or half full after the night before.
The Hotel is attached to the Bar or vice-versa.
Anyway all is dark – darker for the light outside.

I wait outside in the car and am told on the radio
how to write a Bestseller. Apparently it's hard work
Not like poetry, though he doesn't say that.
Beyond the hour I cannot wait.
The man and the stream are keeping their appointment.

Soon I have to leave the reaching bags, the dark shop,
the tabloid headlines,
the two girls in their purdah of darkness
minding the goods that mark my hysteria;
This village that still knows an emergency
as something that only happens in the middle of winter
when the snow is down.
Flu and darkness have taken us hostage out of season.

1973

Eiléan Ní Chuilleanáin was born in Cork in 1942 and educated at University College Cork and at Oxford. She is a Fellow of Trinity College Dublin, where she is an Associate Professor of English and Dean of Arts (Letters). She is also a member of Aosdána. Together with Leland Bardwell, Pearse Hutchinson and her husband, Macdara Woods, she is a founder editor of the literary review *Cyphers* (1975).

She has seven collections of poetry: *Acts and Monuments* (1972), *Site of Ambush* (1975), *The Second Voyage* (1977), *The Rose Geranium* (1981), *The Magdalene Sermon* (1989), *The Brazen Serpent* (1994) and *The Girl Who Married the Reindeer* (2001). In Ireland she is published by The Gallery Press, in the UK by Bloodaxe Books and in America by Wake Forest University Press. The Irish-American Cultural Institute awarded her the O'Shaughnessy Prize for Poetry in 1992.

Two poems here, 'In the Hills' and 'The Married Women', have not been collected previously. Eiléan has a son, Niall, and lives in Dublin.

Bessboro

This is what I inherit –
It was never my own life,
But a house's name I heard
And others heard as warning
Of what might happen a girl
Daring and caught by ill-luck:
A fragment of desolate
Fact, a hammer-note of fear –

But I never saw the place.
Now that I stand at the gate
And that time is so long gone
It is their absence that rains,
That stabs right into the seams
Of my big coat, settling
On my shoulder, in pointed
Needles, crowding the short day.

The white barred gate is closed,
The white fence tracks out of sight
Where the avenue goes, rain
Veils distance, douses all sound
And a halfdrawn lace of mist
Hides elements of the known:
Gables and high blind windows.
The story has moved away.

The rain darns into the grass,
Blown over the tidal lough
Past the isolated roof
And the tall trees in the park;
It gusts off to south and west;
Earth is secret as ever:
The blood that was sown here flowered
And all the seeds blew away.

Agnes Bernelle

There is no beast I love better than the spider
That makes her own new centre every day
Catching brilliantly the light of autumn,

That judges the depth of the rosemary bush
And the slant of the sun on the brick wall
When she slings her veils and pinnacles.

She crouches on her knife edge, an ideogram combining
The word for *tools* with the word for *discipline*,
Ready for a lifetime of cold rehearsals;

Her presence is the syllable on the white wall,
The hooked shadow. Her children are everywhere,
Her strands as long as the railway-line in the desert

That shines one instant and the next is doused in dust.
If she could only sing she would be perfect, but
In everything else she reminds me of you.

In Her Other House

In my other house all the books are lined on shelves
And maybe taken down in a curious mood.
The postman arrives with letters to all the family,
The table is spread and cleared by invisible hands.

It is the dead who serve us, and I see
My father's glass and the bottle of sour stout at hand
Guarding his place (so I know it cannot be real;
The only boy with six sisters never learned

To set a table, though books lined up at his command.)
In this room with a fire, books, a meal and a minute
When everyone is out of sight washing their hands,
A man comes through the door, shedding his coat;

He turns like a dancer before it touches the ground,
Retrieving a lily from somewhere. Where he has been,
You turn out your pockets every time a door is opened;
But the flower has travelled with him and he is in safe hands –

On the shelf a letter for him flashes a wide bright stamp.
He mutters once more, *Here goes, in the name of God* –
Women's voices sound outside, he breathes deeply and quickly
And returns to talk to the fire, smiling and warming his hands –

In this house there is no need to wait for the verdict of history
And each page lies open to the version of every other.

In Her Other Ireland

It's a small town. The wind blows past
The dunes, and sands the wide street.
The flagstones are wet, in places thick with glass,
Long claws of scattering light.
The names are lonely, the shutters blank –
No-one's around when the wind blows.

The mistress of novices has sent all the novices
Upstairs into the choir to practise
The service for deliverance from storms and thunder.
Their light dapples the sharkskin windows,
The harmonium pants uphill,
The storm plucks riffs on the high tower.

And on the fair green the merry-go-round
Whistles and whirls. The old man has joined
His helper on the plinth. He calls his son
To throw him a rope, and watch for a loosening
Strut or a pelmet or the whole wheel
Spinning lifting and drifting and crashing.

But it spins away, grinding up speed,
Growling above the thunder. The rain
Has begun again; the old man's helper,
Darkfaced with a moustache, holds on.
They try to slow it with their weight,
Calling to the youngster to hang on the rope;

It's a small town, a small town;
Nowhere to go when the wind blows.

Inheriting the Books

They've come and made their camp
Within sight, within slingshot,
A circle of bulked shapes
Dark inside like wagons.
There are fires like open eyes.
I watch the billows of smoke,
The dark patches, hallucinating
Herds and horses.

Who is that in flashing garments
Bowing to the earth over and over,
Is it a woman or a child?
In the wedge of the valley by the stream
What food are they cooking, what names have they
For washing the dead, for the days of the week?

The long rope has landed, the loose siege hemming me.
In whatever time remains, I will not have the strength to depart.

In the Hills

1

You are almost at the end of your journey
And nobody has asked you for help
Since the child playing by the yellow gable
Who had lost her ball in the gully.
The broad linked chain still weighs down your pocket.

It is early in the mountains,
The mist thronged like blossom,
The grassy road to the harbour
Grey with dew, the branches
Loaded like a bride with embroidery.

2

Do you remember the dark night
When the voice cried from the yard
Asking for water, and you rose from the bed.
You were gone so long, I said to myself at last
As long as I live I will never ask who was there.

But now I want to ask that question.
I see you at the boundary stone and I need
To say the word that will bring her out of the trees:
Notice her: she limps to the field's edge:
A step, a clutch at the baldric, a hand to her hair.

The little stony stream divides forest from field.
She looks away. The wooded scene accentuates
The grace that says *look – don't look* wavering
Like the spring breeze tossing the leaves, her draperies
Hesitant, her flexed foot on dappled gravel.

The Married Women

Yes. But you can have no idea
What she was running from,
Feared far more than the convent with its high stairs

It was those women with their bangles
Their stiff new hats at Easter
Their weddings and honeymoons in the Channel Islands.

Their daughters had ponies, the husbands
Had business and whiskey. Their hair
Was crimped in salons, they met each other for coffee

In town after ten Mass. To the child
They seemed made out of timber and steel,
Stiffened by a dose that had penetrated their flesh,

Poisoned and tinged them lightly purple.
She avoided them all her life:
Then on a Monday morning in a pool dressing-room

She saw a woman, that timber face
Her towel as brisk as ever, her jeans
So stiff and brisk on their hook she thought of the new hats.

The woman turned, and under the towel
As if shrouded by the mantled oxter
Of a heroic bird, was a girl's mother-of-pearl sheen,

A girl's hesitant body, protected by the bird's broad wing.

1974

Paul Durcan was born in Dublin in 1944. His first
collection of poems, *Endsville*, co-authored with Brian Lynch,
appeared in 1967. Since then he has published seventeen
others, including *Teresa's Bar* (The Gallery Press 1976,
revised 1986), *The Selected Paul Durcan* (edited by Edna
Longley, The Blackstaff Press 1982), *Jumping the Train
Tracks with Angela* (Raven Arts Press and Carcanet Press
1983), *The Berlin Wall Café* (Blackstaff 1985), *Going Home
to Russia* (Blackstaff 1987), *Crazy about Women* (The
National Gallery of Ireland 1991) and *Cries of an Irish
Caveman* (The Harvill Press 2001). *Daddy, Daddy* (Blackstaff
1990) won the Whitbread Poetry Award. *A Snail in My
Prime, New and Selected Poems*, was published by Harvill
and Blackstaff in 1993.

The first two poems reprinted here are from *O Westport in
the Light of Asia Minor* (Anna Livia Press 1975) and the third
from *Greetings to Our Friends in Brazil* (Harvill 1999). In
2003 *Paul Durcan's Diary*, a collection of his RTÉ Radio 1
broadcasts, was brought out by New Island Books. Paul
Durcan lives in Dublin.

Photo credit: Derek Speirs

Nessa

I met her on the First of August
In the Shangri-La Hotel,
She took me by the index finger
And dropped me in her well.
And that was a whirlpool, that was a whirlpool,
And I very nearly drowned.

Take off your pants, she said to me,
And I very nearly didn't;
Would you care to swim, she said to me,
And I hopped into the Irish Sea.
And that was a whirlpool, that was a whirlpool,
And I very nearly drowned.

On the way back I fell in the field
And she fell down beside me,
I'd have lain in the grass with her all my life
With Nessa:
She was a whirlpool, she was a whirlpool,
And I very nearly drowned.

O Nessa my dear, Nessa my dear,
Will you stay with me on the rocks?
Will you come for me into the Irish Sea
And for me let your red hair down?
And then we will ride into Dublin City
In a taxi-cab wrapped up in dust.
Oh you are a whirlpool, you are a whirlpool,
And I am very nearly drowned.

November 30, 1967
to Katherine

I awoke with a pain in my head
And my mother standing at the end of the bed;
'There's bad news in the paper,' she said,
'Patrick Kavanagh is dead.'

After a week which was not real
At last I settled down to a natural meal;
I was sitting over a pint and a beef sandwich
In Mooney's across the street from the Rotunda.

By accident I happened to tune in
To the conversation at the table from me;
I heard an old Northsider tell to his missus
'He was pure straight, God rest him, not like us.'

Waterloo Road

On Waterloo Road on an August day
I met Patrick Kavanagh in his garden flat.
After I rang the bell there was a long pause –
To open … or not to open –
Before I identified two sad, wise, humorous eyes
In black horn
Peering out at me through the spyhole window high up in
     the door.

Patrick Kavanagh led me up the long hall
To the living-room at the back looking out on the garden.
He sat down in an ocean-going armchair of a past era
With dozens of anthologies of American poetry
In stacks round about his shoeless feet on the floor.
He blinked up into the skies behind me:
'The American anthology is great for the kickstart.'
We sat in silence – two deferential elephants.
He the old cobbler at the term of his days;
I the young apprentice in my first pregnancy.
'The apprenticeship,' he declared eagerly, sitting out forward
'The apprenticeship, you know, is twenty years.'

It was a golden day on Waterloo Road –
Blue skies, shirt sleeves, bicycles, miniskirts –
As we strolled down to the Waterloo House
Past Michael Kane's big window for a lunchtime drink.
There was an anticyclone over Ireland.
At the construction site on the corner of Waterloo Road
That was to become the office block of the Yellow Pages
Patrick Kavanagh halted with his hands on his hips
Gazing up at the meteoric men in yellow hats
Walking tightropes smoking fags.
From them to me he switched gaze solemnly.
Divining the mystery of the universe, he announced:
'Men at Work!' He tossed his head back. 'Men at Work!'

That day Patrick Kavanagh had a wedding to go to
In the Shangri-La Hotel on the hill of Dalkey.

Through the armies of the sun we rode a taxi
Like Lenny Bruce and Billy the Kid
In a chariot along the shore of Dublin Bay.
Although I was homeless, jobless, futureless,
I felt wholly safe in Patrick Kavanagh's company.
I uttered: 'Today is such a golden day
It reminds me of days I stayed in the monastery –
The Trappist Monastery at Mount Melleray.'

Consternation in the back of the taxi.
Patrick Kavanagh groaned:
'On a summer's day like today
Don't be thinking about monasteries.
On a summer's day like today
You should be thinking about beautiful women.'
When in the lobby of the Shangri-La
The head waiter spotted us
He took us for a pair of winos,
Made to throw us out,
Only for the bridegroom to rescue us.
Patrick Kavanagh was the guest of honour.

Humming snatches of 'On Raglan Road'
Patrick Kavanagh sat down on a couch behind me –
'For that I'll vouch on any couch' –
While I, sitting up at the bar, found
Myself beside a beautiful woman
With long red hair, green eyes, freckles.
Nessa O'Neill was her name and she invited me
To go for a swim with her at the bottom of the garden.
The Shangri-La backed on to the Irish Sea.
There was an Indian Summer that year in Ireland
And in October she and I set up home in London.
We lived together sixteen years,
Rearing two golden girls.

On Waterloo Road on the first of August I met her first and knew
That her red hair would weave a snare that I would never rue;
I embraced the danger, I sailed along in the enchanted cab
And I rowed my oar by the star of Patrick Kavanagh.

1975

John Ennis, PhD, is head of the School of
Humanities at Waterford Institute of Technology. He was an
executive member of Poetry Ireland from 1979 to 1990 and
has edited *Poetry Ireland Review*. He has eleven collections
of poetry: *Night on Hibernia* (1976), *Dolmen Hill* (1977), *A
Drink of Spring* (1979) and *The Burren Days* (1985), all
published by The Gallery Press; *Arboretum* (1990), *In a
Green Shade* (1991), *Down in the Deeper Helicon* (1994),
Telling the Bees (1995), *Selected Poems* (1996), *Traithnini*
(2000) and *Near St. Mullins* (2002), all published by The
Dedalus Press. *Goldcrest Falling* will be published by Scope
Productions in 2004. He is also joint editor with Stephanie
McKenzie of *The Backyards of Heaven: An Anthology of
Contemporary Poetry from Ireland and Newfoundland &
Labrador* (2003), which included poems by eighteen
winners of the Patrick Kavanagh Poetry Award. John Ennis
has won the Listowel International Open Poetry Competition
on eleven occasions and was the recipient of the Irish-
American Cultural Institute Award in 1996.

The first poem here is from *Night on Hibernia*, based on the
collection that won the Patrick Kavanagh Poetry Award.

Sgarúint na gCompánach

Abruptly, soon after breakfast, you departed, food
Gulped, at dawn this morning. Cratered moon petered
Out at its zenith. Cold fists of blue deterred
Clouds from the sky. I had meant to say good
Bye offering a gift by which no heaven, hell
Would separate us ever. When I knocked, no
    reply
Helloed. Running downstairs I saw the car already
Take you. A few hands were raised in farewell.

I walked upstairs, went in your room. In it cruel disarray:
Smells of the bitter afterbirth, your sudden removal
Out of our lives. On your bed I sat, saw it all:
Christmas in Clough '62, skating on its frozen lakes in bleak array;
June '63 torrential showers, the daft seas, waves we wore
Clothes tucked under stonewalls; precious rock-haunt lures;
Spirit of Connemara, Torc, the greenwood tours.
I closed the door on what could be no more.

This chilled day of autumn oaks I found no peace at all.
First frosts have inflamed the close September leaves.
Constant in its garish space my mind bleeps, grieves.
Your absence haunts. That speeding car. I recall
Your face at my door, asking a request,
Hard confidences uttered at the end,
That extraordinary flair for etching: when your Christ
Became you at the lintel. I did not comprehend.

I rose, dressed at small hours. 'Am I my brother's guardian?'
And I had dreamt one in sweat. Black soured caws of crows
Streamed round their creaking beech. Leaves beat my window's
Vitreous face. I saw your model aeroplane crash. Cain
Threw wide the salt-raw wound my room in cold harangues.
Without, two joy-drunk hares sported (as our last night
Died). Lawn was all theirs. Clouds veiled the moon.
                             Delight
Exulted: one tumbled, ravished the other. No jaws
    bared fangs.

Henry, accept this pale proffered In Memoriam.
I heard you once cry anger at all ritual
(As we polished gold chalices of the lamb)
That gilds the speechless throat, each
    cleavered call.
These lines cut us somewhat in cross-section,
Engrave the blank metal plates with what was sure.
I tidy your drawing board too, our affection.
Translate your love into life's architecture.

James

Last blue, blue hours, cousin, I hugged you in the flesh
Laughing, a Sunday you cycled February northerly for company.
Cold had slashed rusty scalpels across the sun's face for days.
Hurley strapped to the crossbar, you cycled to me.

Afternoon reinforced all-black ice in tanks. You helloed my parents
Blew indoors, ran out of the book-worm hearth-blazing house.
To the back of it, James, in the hay-strewn sandpit field
We hallowed off nine frozen cattle, two lean bleak dry cows.

You stood sentry one hundred-yards goal, I slope opposite,
We kept no track of scores. Shots echoed. Sounded axes
Sunken in wood. Laughter, till our two throats burnt sore,
Mimicked the once wintry courtships of the silver foxes.

Chairing in for supper, we thought words so beyond the beyond
My grey father across asking after health of yours. You said,
'Great, thanks!' Blue eyes met mine. You choke nowadays on
Mouthfuls browner than floury soda-bread or any wheaten bread.

Adolescents. We were same age. Ungovernable, a raw gaiety
Shook us. Last supper. The house was infectious,
Our mutual lean-to. A thin diluted sunset
Illuminated bread, plates, cups, knives, us.

Starlings flocked twilight in loose neap-dark waves across us.
We palmed rounds of handball against the southern gable
Breaths dawdling white, soft, gauzing the self-sharpening air.
Mad to get out we'd rushed, sprung free of the irrational table.

So caught up, engrossed in our twin scores, I forgot
A pond hollow thickly iced down our indigo forgefield.
Night in soundless little-glittering moonlight, I skated for us.
Five months later I huddled back from you. And still I am not
    steeled.

By August, killed and coffined, you rotted in Coralstown.
Cousin, hour you bled, I searched a cloud-stanched sky
Miles off. I did not know at all that you had died.
I felt savagely on edge. Loss I could not identify.

Hurley strapped fast, you got set to race the dark home. 'So
Long,' waved back to me southward on Murtagh's Hill. Down
Hightown whistling under a snow-clad moon. You cut out on the
    Dublin-Galway
Arterial Road. Yes, we laughed a lot. Good-bye, James,
    Corbetstown.

Against the Wood

When we first settled in by Knockeen wood, I felt its branches
Overpowering of a twilight as I walked its sorrelled innards.
On the third day, in the heat, an old badger dying in a stench
Of maggots dragged himself over our stone wall. He'd been
 snared.

The gloom of trunks is always alive, unique, salient with
 shadows.
The tall plantation steals the sun on us. Even our high
 summers.
Scald crows bed here, magpies chatter, thrushes sway on
 star-topped spruce.
Last August a barn owl cried and cried into the early hours.

From my study I hear the Ballybeg schoolchildren orienteer
On church holidays. The scout-cubbed young from homes
 work has forsaken
Call across the shrub-besieged houses from rock to rock.
Foxes no hunt scares bare their teeth in the high briar.

The summit grows impenetrable to lunge of horse or hound.
Inhaling the larch and pine to cleanse my sunset mind,
I've walked ten thousand times round its berried mount.
Storms fell trees at the edges now. I feel my own days sway
 in the wind.

Old histories lie buried here, old walls, old gables, by green
 moss.
Lichens struggle for the sun on floors of dead leaves, bitter
 ivies.
In the beginning, I filled up hempen sacks, yes, old deciduous
Sacks for compost in cold stanzaic frames to raise new
 boundaries.

Coolness in heat. Shelter in black wind. Sanctuary. O sweet
 resin.
In July the night lightning is magnificent across the white
 forest.

And each May, beneath greening canopies, there's that other
    firmament,
I remember my first astonishment at bluebells and their blue
    aura –

How they filled with an inviolable cadence the noonday
    woodside,
How the bees dared long, for the nectar, into their low gloom,
How it was sacrilege to march, or doubt, across that young tide,
How their short translucence sang out with voices for our
    time.

Illumination

The cart is stacked with sheaves for the haggard,
    the ropes are stretched taut
and knotted at the base of the shafts. In the mountain field,
    the height
that gave a view of Wicklow crests, the terrier barks less
in the flattened circle
of stubble that was a sheaf stack. He snags the mother mouse down
    in one gulp.
His paw uncovers – or is it the gleaming pitchfork? – the clean
    chaffy nest with four
baby mice, pink, hairless and delicate, faintly moving,
    where a furrow home
ran lately with breeding spaces and the curves of oats divided in gold
once at the end of August in a warm wind when the idea
    of a home was considered.

After the barking, the laughing, the shouting, the last stack,
    they are looking down, three of
my brothers from their cargo of corn. Astride the sheaves
    in uncustomary silence. The full moon rises
over O'Hara's. Oval as a face and still, pure orange. The cart creaks,
    sways away into the twilight.

Your faces have grown pale. A wind stirs. Hint of later frost?
    Mist? Fog at daybreak?
The threshing's near. I linger by the quiet forms a half-hour or more
    till I am called.
On my hunkers under a clear October night. The last to walk away
    from the nest.

Vedic

Let all our future poems be dying swans
And may Lilia Musovarova rule them all
As they come on stage for our loved ones:
Let them be, in the main, at their beck and call,

Choreograph the daily griefs, dramas, joys, the little harms
And let them know our love for them is sound:
We that have known the ripple and the wingspan in the arm
The attempts at flight that never leave the ground.

Let us incorporate grace, at once balletic and proud,
The courage of the solo in the words of every poem,
The dancing essences to be soft spoken, or cried aloud,
Fearless of nothing but the loss of those bright waters we call home.

And may these failing birds find resurrection in our wills
Retrace their wings to cygnethood on lakes between the hills.

1976

Aidan Mathews was born in 1956 in Dublin.

His poetry collections include *Windfalls* (The Dolmen Press 1977), *Minding Ruth* (The Gallery Press 1983) and *According to the Small Hours* (Jonathan Cape 1998). His plays are: *The Diamond Body* and *Gone Anti* (The Antigone), the Project Theatre, Dublin, 1984; *Exit Entrance* (1988) and *Communion* (2002), the Peacock Theatre, Dublin; and a translation of *The House of Bernard Alba* (1989), the Gate Theatre, Dublin. He has also two collections of stories, *Adventures in a Bathyscope* (1988) and *Lipstick on the Host* (1992), and a novel *Muesli at Midnight* (1990), all published by Secker and Warburg of London. He won the Macaulay Fellowship in 1978/9 and an Academy of American Poets Award in 1982. He lives in Co. Dublin.

'Returning to Kilcoole' is from *Windfalls*, which won the Patrick Kavanagh Poetry Award; the other four poems here are from a new collection, *Politics of an Idiot.*

Returning to Kilcoole

Hubcaps, horsedroppings rubble the sand.
Although I had managed to remember
The fabulous frenzy of alarmed snipe,
Hedges brown as a smoker's fingers,
The railway track was foremost in my mind.

Often in my eagerness I anklesprained
Among those rails, was always terrified
Of trains running me over, had nightmares
Full of broken skulls, revolving wheels.
I used go there with my godfather
Who had a blackthorn and noticed everything.

I grew up to his hip, elbow, shoulder:
Then it was time to begin remembering
Important things. The heron we both saw
Through his binoculars when I was twelve

And informed him it was a flamingo;
Or the time we were there around midnight

To hear the ocean perspiring and blacker
Than tar. I suppose I was about fourteen
And needed to be alone and so we put
Two hundred yards between the two of us.
I think we were closer then than ever before.

At the Junction

There is the hum of car-windows closing.
Even the sunroofs slip shut with a sigh
As refugees at the red light infiltrate
The lane discipline of our stalled drive-time.

Some brat of an Indo-European lavishes
Lather on my own clean windscreen.
The wipers stop, stuck in the slush,
Like the wartime whitewashed window-panes

Of a tram that crossed through the Warsaw ghetto.
But I won't be blackmailed by sob stories,
I who drive an economy Opel
From outpatients to outpatients,

A middle-aged manic depressive male
Whose gifts at the altar are all
Wafer-thin, watered down, tactical;
And who hardly remembers the time or the day

When Masahiko from Tokyo came
To a Cabinteely cul-de-sac
And the children there queued up in a line
To stroke his goatee beard like a bell-rope,

Its sleek silvery Shinto softness
Shining and winding its way down
To where I could see the paw-prints of infants,
A moon looming over a hangnail.

Imperial War Museum

Watching a war-film with you
A week before you die,
I remember only embarrassment
The time you lifted me down
Inside a spitfire's cockpit
As an ex-serviceman smiled.

At the military parade
For the 1916 Rising,
Spitfires stooped on O'Connell Street.
I held onto your sleeve among
Veterans' urinous trouserlegs,
Lapels with metal tricolours.

While you were performing maybe
A corporectomy, was it,
I glued a spitfire together
From a plastic skeleton kit
And landed it on your bureau.
That won't get you into college,

To Biggin Hill or Biggles.
How many bones in the hand?
How many hands in the pot?
Make a fist of your hand while you can!
But now your finger is shaking
Like a boy's touching a breast

As you point at the battle of Britain
On the set with too many ad breaks
Full of beautiful, healing flesh.
So many minor strokes
Have made you half-human again,
Have brought you down to earth

Like the paralysed man in Luke
Let down through the roof by his friends,
No deus ex machina

But a crash-landed pilot
Where the ground gives and forgives
And a parachute lags the immersion.

When you die I will kiss your hand
On its heavy, hardened palm
Where you started a stopped heart
In the operating theatre
Or groomed the underarm hairs
Of the woman I knew as my mother.

Yet watching the war-film with you
Something in us has been heightened –
A wing and a prayer in English,
The flight of father and son –
As I try to talk you down
On your sky-blue final throne.

Decency

Granny's smoking in her sickroom
On the left-hand side of the landing.
Life goes so fast. She can't draw breath.
If I knock at her door she'll be squatting
On a jumbo bale of geriatric diapers.

On the right-hand side of the landing,
The lovely scent of my daughter's urine.
I butter her vulva with cold cream,
Her scorched anus, her dimply bum,
And I parcel her into a sellotaped Pampers.

In the middle, straight before me,
At eye-level, my level, a tacked crucifix.
Jesus in a loincloth on the cross.
What I wondered at fifteen was:
Were they ashamed to show his cock?

Had his cadaver a hard-on?
Was the Church ashamed he'd been docked,
A Jew of the House of Jacob,
Or was it, as the Schoolmen argued,
That he had never defecated?

You live. You learn. Life goes so fast.
Whether swaddling clothes in a stable
Or a linen sheet in the tomb,
There are things so holy they should be hidden –
Those parts of the body that moisten

To disclose fully the flesh and blood
Which haunts us more than metaphysics.
It is our own species we eat and drink
And the odour of sanctity on my hands –
Shit and piss – is a relic of decency.

After Omagh

It was where you turn at the meat processing plant.
I braked for ambulances, police panda cars,
But what exploded there out of the silent cinema
Was a nineteen-twenties vintage model Ford;
A Brylcreemed bridegroom and his Gatsby bride;
Her veil in the vents of the wind like a first-aid dressing,
And the wedding convoy's horns.

They were the treble of school-bells, falsetto all-clears,
The baritone of wild geese from their arctic detour,
Nude picture postcards in an alarmed letter-box;
And they were the howl of the grounds of a great house closing,
The uproar of the primates in the zoo at nightfall,
Or the office fire-drill where I file in shirtsleeves
And the steward lists the missing.

I leaned on my own car-horn until my palm hurt,
Pressing it like the one note of an accordion
In my sound-proofed southern car. The rest is sirens ...
They will leave the queer mirrors of their hotel elevator
To watch the wedding video with the volume turned down
And the soprano in the News for the Deaf at midnight, even,
Will be dumbfounded too at their shapes under a sheet.

1977

Thomas McCarthy, born in Co. Waterford in 1954 and educated at University College Cork, has worked at Cork City Library for many years. He has published six collections of poetry, including *The Sorrow Garden* and *Mr Dineen's Careful Parade*; two novels, *Without Power* and *Asya and Christine*; and has also edited *The Cork Review* and *Poetry Ireland Review*. He won the Alice Hunt Bartlett Prize in 1981, the Ireland Funds Annual Literary Award in 1984 and the O'Shaughnessy Prize for Poetry. His poems have been translated into many languages and have appeared in more than thirty anthologies, among them *Contemporary Irish Poetry* (Penguin Books), *Bitter Harvest* (Scribners) and *Rosa di macchia* (Passagli, Florence). In 1994/5 he was Humphrey Professor of English at Macalester College, Minnesota, USA. Thomas McCarthy is a Fellow of the Royal Society of Arts and a member of Aosdána and of the Board of Poetry Ireland. He is married and has two children, Kate Inez and Neil.

The first poem here is from *The First Convention* (The Dolmen Press 1978), based on the collection that won the Patrick Kavanagh Poetry Award.

Daedalus, the Maker

for Seán Lucy

Dactylos was silent and impersonal;
hidden behind false names, he achieved
a powerful *persona*. There was only
his work; a chipping of rock into form
and the rhythmic riveting of bronze,
diminishing his need for company.

Learning to keep silent is a difficult
task. To place Art anonymously at
the Earth's altar, then to scurry away
like a wounded animal, is the most cruel
test-piece. A proud maker, I have waited at
the temple doors for praise and argument.

Often I have abandoned an emerging form
to argue with priests and poets –
only to learn the wisdom of Dactylos:
that words make the strangest labyrinth,
with circular passages and minotaurs
lurking in the most innocent lines.

I will banish argument to work again
with bronze. Words, I have found, are
captured, not made: opinion alone is
a kind of retreat. I shall become like
Dactylos, a quiet maker; moving between
poet and priest, keeping my pride secret.

Nathaniel Murphy Considers
The Edinburgh Review, 1811

I sit in the worst coffee-house in Castle Street,
Weary with Cork rain, weary with it,
And turn page after page of Mr Jeffrey's disdain
Of everything in the exiled Lord Byron.

Neither the strong and sensual aroma of cups
Or the *milles feuilles* of the *Edinburgh Review*
Can transport us out of the ice-age of age;
Nor can Byron's profligate heartlessness

Lift me out of the invalid's cradle of virtue.
I am weary of the ocean's incorruptible honour
And of ships that bring nobility, casket
After casket. Turning these pages, I cannot wish

To be reconciled. I, also, remember the intrigues
Of Italy, the sweet illusions of Rome.
My coffee cup upon the mantel-piece leaves its ring
The way Italy leaves its taste upon my tongue.

Mr Nathaniel Murphy in His Sister's Bedroom, 1798

When my sister ran away with Polyphemus Shea –
A clerk from the quayside Custom House
Who promised her a life of Art in Boston –
She abandoned her cherrywood escritoire in the cave
Of her bedroom. My father's gift it was,
Made by the cabinet-maker O'Connell.

Like a buckle-thief
In Paul Street
I have removed the silver plate
With her names: *Letitia Louise.*

My only sister, so dear to me –
As far from her native Irish Kingdom
As Mr Singleton Copley is
From the quays of Jacobin New England.

Lady Nora Wingfield, Mrs Nat Hutchins, Lady Keane

I am sitting among the artichokes with the head gardener
Who keeps singing *The Green, Green Grass of Home*
With the passion of a man who has been stabbed
By an iron-toothed rake. I have coaxed the damp earth
Into a fine tilth, and the afternoon sun has come
Back again after a brief mishap of July rain.
Faraway from me now in the narrower room
Of adult life, I can still tell their voices apart.
I can hear Lady Nora's voice and Lady Keane's
Quick answer, her tone as controlled as the pure glaze
On Meissen. They are talking about Ulster –
Nothing troublesome, mind you, but flowers:

Mount Stewart rhododendrons, the hybrid *Lady Alice FitzWilliam*
And a border plant as pink and delicate as old porcelain.
Mrs Nat Hutchins approaches me for a bowl of cut globes
And I, as sensitive to her needs as an Ulster apprentice,
Offer up the filled trug. Unreal, it is. Long ago. To touch them
At all nowadays I need to place my adult hands on the earth
And feel the radical power, the good husbandry,
Of Lady Keane and her friends. Smells of leaf and loam
Are like the sexual taste of the sea, Clonea or Tramore,
To those with a conventional childhood. I'm glad
I never had much of the sea or the sea's companions.

A parish of rich women is what I had instead,
A soirée of readers, their *Received Pronunciation*,
And a chance to see time like a table set for unfinished poems.

Question Time

Question time at the end of another Election Year;
Senators and their wives dancing on the ballroom floor;
children in corners dropping crisps and cream,
their fathers ordering them home, their mothers in crinoline
having to put them outside to sulk in the Christmas dark.
Enmities dissolving now in a sea of drink and smoke and talk.

Who was Robert Emmet's mistress? Who was Kitty O'Shea?
Which IRA man was shot on his own wedding-day?
How many death-warrants did Kevin O'Higgins sign?
So much to answer between the buffet meal and wine –
But the prize is a week in Brussels, money for two,
and kisses from two Euro-MPs just passing through.

1978

Rory Brennan was born in Westport, Co. Mayo, in

1945 but grew up and went to school in Dublin where he
attended Trinity College. He taught for two years in
Casablanca, Morocco, and has since travelled widely in
North Africa, the Far East, the US and Europe, spending
extended periods in Greece on one of the Cycladic islands.
He lives in Dublin and has worked as a broadcaster in RTÉ,
as director of Poetry Ireland and as a lecturer and reviewer;
currently he is a lecturer in Communications at Dublin City
University. He is married to Fionnuala and they have two
grown-up daughters. Rory Brennan has published three
collections of poetry.

The first two poems here are from *The Sea on Fire* (The
Dolmen Press 1979), which won the Patrick Kavanagh
Poetry Award; the next three are from *The Walking Wounded*
(The Dedalus Press 1985); and the final three are from *The
Old in Rapallo* (Salmon Poetry 1996).

This Knotted Cord

All children play with string
And tie it into knots. The child
Gets tired, takes up some other thing.
But I kept on, I was beguiled

By close-knit things that came apart,
That could be reassembled, understood –
All this unravelling is not art
Unless the tying-up again is good.

This compulsion that I tried to kill,
This knotted cord, this noose of words,
Wound round my throat and strangles still.
I dance to keep my feet upon the boards.

Security

A journey does not imply a return.
Columbus' sailors, starved and cold,
Feared sailing over the rim of the world.
Security is having boats to burn.

The Oil Lamp

I hear the bamboo creak like a cracked joint
Although the terrace stays so still-life still.
The oil lamp's blade is pared to a fine point
And purrs inside its glass. A long tendril
Wavers like a signal from its clouded stack.
The crickets tune non-stop their lost waveband
Deciphering a code they cannot crack
With only one glazed star to lend a hand …
A still scenario a good painter could
Catch all the silence in but not that creak
That has the nervy twang of brittle wood.
With a deep breath the decamped wind is back.
I look in at the window with a start:
The lantern's blade is jabbing at my heart.

The Threshing Circles

It seems as if a giant coin was flipped
And spun three times, striking the hill
And stamping it with stone lipped
Perfect circles as it plunged and fell.
Miniature ring forts with broken teeth
For ramparts, trampling their floors
Horses in late summer churn a froth
Of chaff, a tent of golden filings in the air
To shelter them, gone absent without leave
From the massed ranks of myth. At night
The threshing circles rise again, have
Three counterparts that spatter light,
The bracelets of three villages that make
Circles like camp-fires or birthday cakes.

The Other Islands

Are mostly never there. A mosquito net of haze
Hangs loose offshore and wraps us lazily
In a steam bath horizon. It takes a blaze
Of sun in a stripped bare sky to see
The other mountain tops beyond our own
And be surprised again how self-contained
It's possible to be, or that to be alone
We can take too easily for granted like a friend.
I do not know their names – they end in -os
And certainly have favourite gods and crops,
A port and inland villages, places to visit,
Places I may have been – I need a map
Because I take on trust what lies so close
And for a change feel no strong need to name it.

The Paper Kisses

A secret invasion of cherubs was what it was like,
This littering of the house with impressions of lips,
Immaculately printed, love's own personal calling cards,
Ghost-mouths whispering inaudible promises,
Ripe beauty hinted in their Cupid's bows.

Pink, mauve, rosé, ochre, vermillion, deep red,
Their shades could match some prism of the moods
Fired by first love's blinkering firework display.
The paper kisses were so perfect as to seem great art,
Fugitive sketches from a Primavera folio.

But they were planted on old bills, junk mail, torn envelopes,
Flyleaves of paperbacks, runic scraps of their father's foolscap,
Mingling with last demands, free offers, blurbs and poems,
Gracing the quotidian with their luscious blooms,
Reminding us we are insubstantial and forgotten without love.

Mostly they were to be found near mirrors and telephones
Where hectic lipstickings took place before the dash
To disco, rave, club, bar. Only these last minute dabbings
Were the departure signals of our lovely daughters.
May those who kiss their lips earn their warm hearts.

The Wind Messages
In Memory of Anne Kirwan

Dear Anne, from a seawrack of memories, just two:
First, a sun-kindled bay and a small yellow boat,
A sudden offshore gust had carried you far out ...
That time the ploys of nature did no harm
And you sailed back with sixteen years of life,
And life, exuberantly, was always what you gave.
But in that frail inflatable death dropped a lethal hint.
Next, the summer of eighty-five. You left our house
High on its hill as a brief southern sunset fell
And walked, laughing with friends, down the long slope.
Then far below, by some ventriloquism of the wind,
Through a gap in a toppling dry-stone wall,
Your voice was snatched and swept back up the hill,
Like a bird bearing a message of love in its beak.
Now you are forever out of earshot and a flash flood
Has swallowed up your brain and uprooted all our lives.
Yet above the deluge we still hear your voice. Dear Anne.

Elsewhere and Clonmacnoise

In Memory of Conleth Ellis

Like all the cherished dead you are always with us
And will never abscond, though our grief might wish it.
Only with other deaths will you shyly quit the world
And even then your poems like cloud and river
Will exchange their elaborate evening secrets.
Sunset, all too surely, was your time of day.

But your own cherishing heart is all too dead
And we are appalled it is erased as utterly
As the myriad interlacings of so much memory
Or that vista of sudden rapture we call imagination.
Your arteries had no right to silt up and garotte
A bloodstream driven by such generous beats.

Classroom, rostrum, desk – the screech of chalk
Howls across thirty years. You stand at the blackboard.
Grey-suited and far too young to be enlisted again
In the siegeplan of schools. Branches flexed at the window.
Leonardo might have sketched or Mozart played
To small avail with us. But I hear you holding forth.

The Rathmines Road in nineteen fifty-nine,
All Ireland a faded postcard! But definition returned
Beamed to a larger screen, old teacher became firm friend
When long later the identikit clicked in your rueful smile.
What sidesteps us into the steep impasse of words?
In your obituary I wrote, *he taught three poets.*

Down a pilgrimage road straight as a saint's staff
We once drove towards Clonmacnoise, our tyres
Outracing the trudge of centuries, your talk lightly
Treading in Latin and Irish. With finest scholars from –
Let's pick and choose – Iona, Antioch, Kiev,
You'd hold a fair debate and hold your own.

But you had to learn the stunning inadequacy of brilliance,
So savage since the truth came shining from your hands,
And had to watch, like someone stumbling into a bad play,
The slick win a round of death-rattle applause,
The talentless pander and tout for the driest grain
Of praise or notice. Such famine relief you refused.

The country schoolmaster with integrity! How well
You came to recognize the lies of your own land,
What lay behind the hillocks in cultivated landscapes.
You trusted us to know our trade and were wrong.
How many less intent souls would have called it a day?
Slowly your books came to light like unearthed texts.

At your funeral I could picture you starting to smile,
Arms folded across your chest, half-glancing down,
Leaning against a pillar, a mild sardonic grin
Puckering your lips at the tiring orotundities
Of these uncanny proceedings, honing a barb of wit.
But death is a poor hand at jokes against himself.

When you flew in a small plane over Serengeti
The years must have seemed like fleeing antelope,
Way back to the evenings of hard-earned early poems
When bells had clanged and schoolyards eddied out.
If I have lost your postcard from Mombasa I have kept
Like title deeds the trust you stored in words.

Now you are borne to mind in a saga of elsewheres
But most of all in the chancel at Clonmacnoise,
The late sun hoisting its slashed pennant on the water
As if waiting for the shields of a Norse longboat
To ignite a slain skald's pyre. Elsewhere and always,
By and beyond river and ruined arch, so you remain.

1979

Michael Coady was born in 1939 in Carrick-on-Suir,
Co. Tipperary, where he still lives. He has worked as a
teacher, musician and writer. Bursaries from An Chomhairle
Ealaíon/The Arts Council enabled him to travel in
Newfoundland and the US in the eighties. He has published
four collections with The Gallery Press: *Two for a Woman,
Three for a Man* (1980), based on the collection that won
the Patrick Kavanagh Poetry Award; *Oven Lane* (1987); *All
Souls* (1997); and *One Another* (2003). In both *All Souls* and
One Another he has integrated poetry, prose and his own
photographs in works of overall thematic unity. *Full Tide*, a
miscellany of prose, poetry and illustration, appeared from
Relay Books in 1999. Michael Coady has directed work-
shops, broadcast on radio and television and given readings
at arts events in Ireland and abroad. In 1998 he was elected
a member of Aosdána and in 2004 he received the eighth
annual O'Shaughnessy Award for Poetry. He is married with
three children.

The first poem here is from Michael Coady's first collection,
the next two are from his second and third respectively, and
the final two are from his fourth and most recent.

The Bayonet

Unholy relic of the bleeding mud,
The Somme was where you cut your teeth, I'm told,
My father's uncle brought you back when he
Was pensioned-off with shellshock and with scroll.

We used you as a poker and an axe –
For years you've been entrenched on our hearthstone,
You've stabbed the coal to red, split timber clean
As if the makers meant you for such chores.

I wonder if your heart was ever tempered
In living flesh, wetwarm about your steel?
Your function was the plunge to crimson climax
Of killed and killer coupled, scream on scream.

I know you've soldiered through domestic wars
In all the years you've lain on our hearthstone,
You've seen rage burst and spill about our fire,
You've heard cold-whetted words pierce to the bone.

The dark stains that you bear may be of blood –
When I was young we used to think it so –
But veteran years of cut and thrust and flame
Have breached your battle-edge, unfleshed your core.

Assembling the Parts

Standing in sunshine
by Highway 84
I'm photographing a factory
which is no longer there

looking for my father
by an assembly line
that has halted
and vanished into air

catching the sepia ghost
of a young tubercular Irishman
who's left a rooming house
at 6 a.m. in a winter time
during the Depression

when my mother is still a girl
playing precocious violin,
a Miraculous Medal under
her blouse, in Protestant
oratorios in Waterford.

A pallid face in the crowd
in a dark winter time,
he's coughing in the cold,
assembling typewriters
in Hartford, Connecticut,

waiting for blood on his pillow
to send him home, where he'll
meet her one ordinary
night with the band playing
Solitude in the Foresters' Hall.

Fifty years on
he's nine Septembers dead
and a tourist in sunshine
by Highway 84

is photographing a factory
which is no longer there,

assembling the parts
of the mundane mystery,
the common enigma of journeys
and unscheduled destinations,

the lost intersections
of person and place and time
uniquely fathering everyman
out of the dark.

The Club

You don't realize until you're forty or so
that by then everyone of your age or more
is walking around with some old wound that's buried
back of the eyes or somewhere under the coat.

Even then you forget that some of those you pass
with a nod every day on the road took their hits
quite early on, though you may not remember ever
seeing them stumble or fall or hearing them moan

since that was before the water cleared to show
that wounding seems part of some general plan, with rules
that are not just bloody unfair, they're bloody unknown.
Strange how it took so long for the light to dawn

that sooner or later your own due turn would come
to take one in the shoulder or the gut,
entitling you to limp into the club,
a member in good standing, now fully paid-up.

Adhlacadh an Dreoilín [1]

i.m. Michael Hartnett;
Calvary Cemetery, Newcastle West, 16 October 1999

You were a wren in your ways and shapes,
king of the birds that could roost in the holly,
land on a leaf or dart to the light,
drop out betimes and go into hiding –

just as now in your tidy nest
you're home and dry though the heavens open
to spill down on our heads and hearts
the clouds' overflow out in Calvary Cemetery.

Far from us now the day in John B's
we attempted to rise to *An Clár Bog Déil* [2]
on the coat-tails of The Limerick Rake,
and Bacchus sporting with Venus.

I can foretell the past, you said,
and once, when quizzed by a student at Queen's
about where you stood on religion:
I'm a catalyst. But I'm a Roman catalyst.

Little you weigh as they let you down
and you with Ó Bruadair under your belt
along with Haicéad and Ó Rathaille
and all your own hatchings in our two tongues.

When you're tucked away we traipse back to town,
chastened stragglers of the standing army
with west Limerick mud on our soles and uppers,
agus fágaimid siúd mar atá sé. [3]

[1] The Wren's Burial
[2] 'The White Deal Board': eighteenth-century love song
[3] 'And let us say no more of that': refrain of ballad 'The Limerick Rake'

Normal Singing

The day is now well advanced. And yet it is perhaps a little soon for my song. To sing too soon is fatal, I always find. On the other hand it is possible to leave it too late. The bell goes for sleep and one has not sung.
Winnie: *Happy Days*

The piano reclines in the bar's back room
where in all of its nights and days
it never knew caress
or climax of any kind of sonata.
It's missing two castors behind
and so leans back at its ease
in a corner where drinkers pass
to and fro with bladders full or relieved.

On the piano and around the room
are eleven pots of exotic flowers
that winter or summer never
need watering, and in the bar are seven
more pots of the same.

Over it all is Ellen, who has stood
by an open grave in her time
to see husband and son go down
and almost followed them there
on the wintry day she collapsed
in the yard and was out for the count
two hours on her own. Following which

she fought her way back and after six months
dusted off pots of flowers and threw
the front door open again
to people and drink and singing

for this is a house where lifetimes
of tipsy songs have been sung
and a place for the singsong still,
while the laid-back piano with flowers
just sits in the back room and listens.

It's taken for granted here
that every woman and man
must harbour some kind of a song

and if you should happen
to stumble or lose your way
then you'll be forgiven,
or helped along if anyone
else knows the words.

On New Year's Eve the bar is full
with spillover into the room
of the waterless flowers
and laid-back piano, with songs
all around and tactful calls
now and then for a bit of hush.

Ellen's behind the bar, with Sheila
and Tommy and Margaret assisting,
and women done up to the nines for
the night that's in it. Colour it simple

and sacred, this mortal occasion
of souls assembled to mark
the flux between all that is gone,
and all the unknown to come.

Outside, a steady downpour
advancing from Slievenamon
courses over roof-ridges, slates
and gutters and windows and walls,
streaming down Lough Street, gurgling
into dark drains and off to the river,
then on and on to the sea forever.

As the old year runs out
the back door's unlocked to let it go.
Open the front then to flowing night
and face whatever may come.

Under the plenteous rain
that descends on the valley
midnight strikes on the Town Clock bell
that has measured the hours
for two hundred years

and there, slipping in from the dark,
the poet from Ayr just in time
with his presence as all join hands
and rise to his song together with
millions of others elsewhere
this night of old acquaintance.

Then round the house an exchange of well-wishing,
embraces and kisses and tears
before we return to replenishing glasses
and normal singing continues.

1980

Nuala Archer was born in the US to Irish parents.
A visit to Ireland in the seventies lengthened into a stay of
many years. *Whale on the Line*, based on the collection that
won the Patrick Kavanagh Poetry Award, was published by
The Gallery Press in 1981. She returned to the US in 1984
and in 1986 devoted a special issue of the *Midland Review*
to Irish women's writing. In 1989 she and Medbh
McGuckian brought out a joint collection, *Two Women, Two
Shores* (Baltimore, The New Poets Series, and Salmon
Poetry). *Pan/ama*, a chapbook, was published by Red Dust,
New York in 1992, and in the same year *The Hour of
Pan/ama* was published by Salmon.

Nuala Archer is currently an Associate Professor in the
English Department, Cleveland State University, Ohio. Asked
for a biographical note, she wrote: 'Alive. Living. Loving this
thing called Life. Draw me back Ireland to walk the shores
with yourselves and Hannah Houdini, my red dog,
born flying.'

love to my friends, family, sweethearts and self in ireland

i.

take a squint
see what
they are making
of the critter
there

ii.

I am
struggling
for want
of a change
& a whole –
some excitement

iii.

some of those
snots (old masters)
will yet
slouch back
to study you
& me
sis

iv.

the knit
of identity
that allows
always
for distinction
includes
the drop stitch
&
the pearl

v.

black
irish
an engineer
& gardener
she knows lots
& has lots
to tell
she understands
my desire
to go deep
into woods
& why
they must stay –
the trees

vi.

welloff
is well
off

the barefoot
clown
you know
tickles lips
to speak
for her
through her

vii.

we felt
to each
other
at once

viii.

the murderer
turned out
to be
an unterrified
angel
of kindness
& a messenger
of health

ix.

looking
at us cross-
eyed you
think what
you see is
our deformity
rather
than your own
defect of vision

x.

living
no blame
no shame
she kissed
the smitten mouths
of her own
two centuries

xi.

she made
the vault herself
after
saying
she never could

the beauty is
weconnected

Eight Untitled Suaimhneach Songs

*

Roseate Spoonbills
Lift, henna hair. Pink shadows
   Pull Fall out of Fear.

  **

  I float. Must you throw
  Stones? We are star-debris. Come-
  ET tails in glass.

***

Out the window, names
Multiply. Settle on the
   City. Shems. Shems. S-h-e-ms.

  ****

  Say nothing to me.
  N-u-a-l-a-N-a-d-a-shum-davar.
  A mirror on fire.

*****

Asleep on floating-
Fog-islanded-trees. Asleep
   In your sunset nest.

   ******

   A breeze falls to her
   Knees. Surrenders feet. Turns
   the lingering lay.

****

Bag-of-bricks-sky. Cleave
It with your karate-chop-
Smile. Red birds flying.

* * * * * * * *

- Silence.
    Waters
    From the sun
    Shine,
    Flow tine

- Thunder.
    Water
    Releases
    Harp
    Strings –
    Cat's cradles

- Lightning.
    Your words,
    Water.
    Your love
    A perpetual flame
    In uisce.

1981

Harry Clifton was born in Dublin in 1952 and has
travelled widely in Africa and Asia, as well as more recently
in Europe. He has published five collections of poems with
The Gallery Press: *The Walls of Carthage* (1977); *Office of the
Salt Merchant* (1979); *Comparative Lives* (1982); *The Liberal
Cage* (1988) and *Night Train through the Brenner* (1994).
His recent poems, *God in France: A Paris Sequence 1994–8*,
are published by Metre Editions.

He has been the recipient of fellowships in Germany, France,
the United States and Australia. *The Desert Route, Selected
Poems 1973–88*, published by Gallery in 1992, was a
London Poetry Book Society Recommendation. *On the Spine
of Italy*, his prose study of an Abruzzese mountain commu-
nity, was published by Macmillan in 1999. His short fiction is
collected in *Berkeley's Telephone & Other Fictions* (The
Lilliput Press 2000).

Harry Clifton has taught at Bremen and Bordeaux universi-
ties and at Trinity College Dublin. He divides his time
between France and Ireland.

'Ireland' is from the collection that won the Patrick Kavanagh
Poetry Award.

Photo credit: Pat McGuigan

Ireland

Offshore, islanded
On a sleepless night
At summer's end, this girl and I
Look across at Ireland
As we lie ...

The law ends,
And the sense of time
Over there ... it's a sheltered lee,
Our unsuperintended
Eternity.

Wild seed,
Warrens of breeding
Everywhere ... on the Atlantic side
Graveyards of joyrides,
Used cars.

A ferry
Left some hours ago
For the mainland ... nothing to carry us
Back into history, now,
Until tomorrow.

Moonless
Tides black out the piles
Of the landing-stage ... phosphorescent
Plash of smiles
In darkness

Plays
Between us, in silence
Of fondling, young points growing
Tenderer in violence,
Responding,

But no breakthrough
Into adulthood, no release –

Only merchantmen, destroyers
Riding the breeze
At anchor,

And lights
Across the strait
Winking, calling our adolescence
Into question, as overnight
Ireland waits.

At the Grave of Silone

Lost in the fog at four thousand feet
When the lights come on, I can see them all,
The mountain villages, so small
A blind man feels his way about
Without a stick, and everyone overhears
Everyone else, as they quarrel and shout,
And still they are all alone –
And the places, the years,
Who redeems them? I think again
Of you, Ignazio Silone,
Ten years dead, a hundred miles to the south
On this freezing Apennine chain,
A body interred, forever looking out
On an endlessly fertile plain –

And how we had visited you, one day
When August blew the crops awake
And harvesters toiled, in the drained lake
Of human promise ... Skies were passing away
But nothing had changed on the ground.
Heat and apathy, everyday sound
In your natal village. Unsuccess
With its local dreamers, revving their motorbikes,
Punishing the slot machines.
Fontamara ... it could have been
Aranyaprathet, or Ballaghaderreen.
Without knowing it, we had come to pray
At the shrine of ordinariness –
We, who were running away.

And look at us now, a man and woman
Dodging the Reaper, saving hay
In the high Abruzzo, our window-panes
Rattled by cold, and the sonic vibrations,
Extraterrestrial, superhuman,
Of half a dozen airforce planes
That shatter the peace ... Again, night falls
On this village of limitations

We have come to. Invisible forces spray
Their DUCE-VINCEREMO on our walls.
As your books say,
All of us dream, and stay in thrall
To the usual consolations.
Marriage. America. Going away.

I shut the window, bank the fire,
And pick up Plato on The Good.
The lumberjack, who gives us wood
For nothing, I see him across in the bar
Where a girl is slicing lemons, tidying shelves,
And shadows argue, the porkpie hats
Of failures home from Canada, playing skat
And fourhand poker. Metal crutches,
Phlegm – the man absurdity trails
Like a village dog … If they saw themselves
For just one instant, as they are,
Heroic, but misunderstood,
Their conversations would carry for miles
Like the sound of a shot.

Castelli, Cerqueto, cold San Giorgio
Float in the fog, red atmospheres
Connected to each other, and to here,
Where I link your fate with hers and mine,
Unconsciousness everywhere … Fifty years ago,
In exile, writing *Bread and Wine*,
The War was coming. Now, below your shrine,
Memory tries to wake
Blind monuments to the Fascist dead,
Disheartened villages, men who cannot shake
The ant of toil from their Sunday clothes,
Slatternly women, old for their years,
The Christian cross, the Communist rose,
With the human word you said.

The River

When I was angry, I went to the river –
New water on old stones, the patience of pools.
Let the will find its own pace,
Said a voice inside me
I was learning to believe,

And the rest will take care of itself.
The fish were facing upstream, tiny trout
Suspended like souls, in their aqueous element.
I and my godlike shadow
Fell across them, and they disappeared.

All this happened deep in the mountains –
Anger, trout, and shadow
With the river flowing through them.
Far away, invisible but imagined,
Was an ancient sea, where things would resolve themselves.

1982

Peter Sirr was born in Waterford in 1960 and now lives

in Dublin, where he works as a freelance writer, editor and translator. After graduating from Trinity College he spent a number of years in Holland and Italy, returning to Dublin in 1991 to become the first director of the Irish Writers' Centre, where he remained until 2002. He was a founder editor of the cultural journal *Graph* and is currently editor of *Poetry Ireland Review*. He has published five collections of poetry, all with The Gallery Press.

The first poem reprinted here is from *Marginal Zones* (1984), based on the collection that won the Patrick Kavanagh Poetry Award; the second is from *Talk, Talk* (1987); the third is from *Ways of Falling* (1991); 'Cures' is from *The Ledger of Fruitful Exchange* (1995); and the final poem, 'Peter Street', is from *Bring Everything* (2000).

The King in the Forest

Here a reign endures, among the trees,
Someone's lordship of small noises –
Leaf-tides and birdsong, a fleeing hare's
Diminishing returns, and underfoot
The brittle politics of the forest floor.

Elsewhere battlement and parapet assert
Our so much less than godly rights.
Prince of nothing, antic inheritor
Of everything ungovernable
I venture deep into the forest …

Habitat of the hesitant, where shy
Motions proliferate! Flowers proffer
Nothing comprehensible, fungi observe
Not the least heraldic rule, and the slender
Deer elude me. I am a connoisseur

Of ash-*lied* and oak-elegy, and when
The limbed light comes through the trees
I am the startled interloper set down
In a corner of the canvas, an afterthought
Or a study in perspective, who sees

The leaves transfigured, the thin hands raised.

Vigils

Something of me is still there, held forever
in the white light of a difficult room, the air
all constraint, a thinness; something useless:
a hand lifted into space, getting nowhere,
a word dying in its bed of language

and often I'd turn to you with a righteous magic
turning love to air, hugging grief
like a toy. But lying here this morning
watching the light grow on your cheek
in the seconds I love, before the clock shrieks

and your skinny shoulders come to life
in my palms, I felt something stir, some gentle pressure
as if my father had pushed the air aside
with mild impatience, reaching down the light
to where we lay

Listen to me. Why do you never listen?

'Of the thousand ways to touch you'

Of the thousand ways to touch you
I select this one
the finger running gently
from toe to thigh and back again
its route fixed, like a tram
snug beneath its wires
                              above
my finger now, bolt after bolt of blue fire
rocking the air ...

Cures

For jaundice a stunned bat worn around the waist
until it dies for epilepsy glowworms in a cloth
loosely tied, laid on the stomach
for deafness a lion's ear for melancholy an ostrich
for desire a sparrowhawk, camphor, calandria

For drunkenness a little bitch half-drowned
its head rubbed against the veins
for dimness of the eyes a salve of apple leaves
for dropsy the spindle tree for migraine
aloe, myrrh, poppy oil and flour

For barrenness hazelnuts, convolvulus, water pepper
for baldness bear's grease, ashes of wheaten straw
for the heart storksbill, nutmeg, for the devil mulled copper
for vexation compress of aspen for catarrh tansy
for worms cherry seeds for fever tormentil, honey

Rowans plums sapphire emerald in wine
topaz in a ring to show poison for fleas dried earth
for hatred a doe for silence the sea for pride
alabaster, oak, leopard, the wrecked sun
creeping to its hut, the night hugging and hoarding

its secret alphabets …

Peter Street

I'd grown almost to love this street,
each time I passed looking up
to pin my father's face to a window, feel myself

held in his gaze. Today there's a building site
where the hospital stood and I stop and stare
stupidly at the empty air, looking for him.

I'd almost pray some ache remain
like a flaw in the structure, something unappeasable
waiting in the fabric, between floors, in some

obstinate, secret room. A crane moves
delicately in the sky, in its own language.
Forget all that, I think as I pass, make it

a marvellous house; music should roam the corridors,
joy readily occur, St Valentine's
stubborn heart come floating from Whitefriar street

to prevail, to undo injury, to lift my father from his bed,
let him climb down the dull red brick, effortlessly,
and run off with his life in his hands.

1983

Greg Delanty was born in Cork in 1958 and
attended university there. He now lives in Burlington,
Vermont, where he teaches at St Michael's College.

His collections include *Cast in the Fire* (The Dolmen Press
1986), *Southward* (The Dedalus Press/LSU 1992), *American
Wake* (The Blackstaff Press/Dufour Editions 1995), *The
Hellbox* (Oxford University Press 1998), *The Blind Stitch*
(Carcanet Press 2001 and LSU 2002), and *The Ship of Birth*
(Carcanet 2003). He has published translations of
Aristophanes' *The Suits (The Knights)* and Euripides'
Orestes. He has also edited, with Nuala Ní Dhomhnaill,
Jumping Off Shadows: Selected Contemporary Irish Poetry
and, with Robert Welch, *The Selected Poems of Patrick
Galvin* (both Cork University Press 1995). He is on the edito-
rial board of *Writing Ulster* and serves as consultant editor
for *The History of the Irish Book* (forthcoming from OUP).

Awards include the Allen Dowling Poetry Fellowship (1986),
the Wolfers–O'Neill Award (1993), the Austin Clarke Award
(1996), Poetry Society of England National Poetry
Competition Prizewinner (1999), an Arts Council of Ireland
Bursary (1998–9) and an award from the Royal Literary
Fund (1999).

Striped Ink

I'm smack-dab in the old tabula rasa days, bamboozled
   by the books
adults bow over, musing if their eyes light upon
   the white or black spaces.

*

A boyhood later, still wren-small, on the top
   storey of The Eagle Printing Company,
I see books pour out and believe that if I fish in
   them
I'll catch the salmon of knowledge, tall-taled
   to us at school,
out of the river of words and like Fionn I'll
   taste
my burning hand and abracadabra I'll fathom what's
   below the surface.

*

But if I'm burnt, it's later that day, on my first
   day as floorboy, spaced from fixing leads,
the devils, Fred and Dommy,
   typesetting a new book, dispatch
me down to Christy Coughlan on the box floor
   for a tin of striped ink.

I take the bait and watch floors of labouring women
   and men flit by, caught in the lift's mesh of Xs,
drowned out by the machines' hullabaloo.
   Somehow between floors the elevator conks out
and I'm stuck on my message that I still haven't
   cottoned on to.

The Marriage Stitch

I can't say why rightly, but suddenly it's clear once more
    what holds us together as we sit, recumbent in the old ease
of each other's company, chewing the rag about friends,
    a poem we loved and such-like. Your Portuguese skin,
set off by a turquoise dress, doesn't hinder either.
    But there's something more than tan-deep between us.
I sew a button to a waistcoat you made me, ravelled years ago.
    You hemmed it with the stitch you mend a frock with now.
Our hands, without thought for individual movement, sew in
    and out, entering and leaving at one and the same time.
If truth be told, the thread had frayed between us, unnoticed
    except for the odd rip. But as we sew, love is
in the mending, and though nothing's said, we feel it
    in a lightness of mood, our ease, our blind stitch.

International Call

A hand holds a receiver out a top-storey window
in a darkening city. The phone is the black
old heavy type. From outside
what can we make of such an event?
The hand, which seems to be a woman's,
holds the phone away from her lover, refusing
to let him answer his high-powered business call.
More likely a mother has got one more
sky-high phone bill and in a tantrum warns
her phone-happy son she'll toss the contraption.
A demented widow, having cracked the number
to the afterlife, holds the receiver out
for the ghost of her lately deceased husband.
He's weary of heaven and wants to hear dusk birds,
particularly the excited choir of city starlings.
It's always dusk now, but the receiver isn't held out
to listen to the birds of the Earth from Heaven.
It's the black ear and mouth in the hand of a woman
as she asks her emigrated sisters and brothers
in a distant country if they can hear the strafing,
and those muffled thuds, how the last thud
made nothing of the hospital where they were slapped
into life. The hand withdraws. The window bangs closed.
The city is shut out. Inside now, the replaced phone
represses a moan. Its ear to the cradle
listens for something approaching from far off.

Behold the Brahmany Kite

That the Brahmany Kite shares the name of a god is not improper
with its rufous body the tincture of Varkala's cliffs and white head
   matching the combers.
The kite riffs, banks and spirals; flapping black-tipped wings
that are mighty as the wings of the skate who might be the bird's
   shade in the stilly water.
The Brahmany makes light of the wind and circles the distant salt-
   and-pepper minarets of Odaayam Mosque
rising above the palms and the silence-made-susurrus of the
   Lakshadweep Sea.
Now the kite is a silhouette in the glare of the sun, reminding me of
   vultures
above the hidden Towers of Silence that Patti and I spotted from the
   Hanging Gardens.
They dined off the cadavers of followers of Zarathustra himself.
And in my way I too believe in the kusthi – the sacred thread –
   of the elements
stitching us all together, and would rather the kite pluck the flesh
   from my bones
than I be laid in the dolled-up box of the West. When the time
   comes, imagine me the grub of the Brahmany.
Keep your elegy eye on the bird a day or so. Watch the kite make
   nothing of me.
Then, as I have now, give the Brahmany an almost imperceptible
   nod and turn and go.

The Alien

I'm back again scrutinizing the Milky Way
   of your ultrasound, scanning the dark
       matter, the nothingness, that now the heads say
   is chockablock with quarks & squarks,
gravitons & gravitini, photons & photinos. Our sprout,

who art there inside the spacecraft
   of your ma, the time capsule of this printout,
       hurling & whirling towards us, it's all daft
   on this earth. Our alien who art in the heavens,
our Martian, our little green man, we're anxious

to make contact, to ask divers questions
   about the heavendom you hail from, to discuss
       the whole shebang of the beginning&end,
   the pre-big-bang untime before you forget the why
and lie of thy first place. And, our friend,

to say Welcome, that we mean no harm, we'd die
   for you even, that we pray you're not here
       to subdue us, that we'd put away
   our ray guns, missiles, attitude and share
our world with you, little big head, if only you stay.

1984

Tom O'Malley

Born in 1942 in a Mayo village on the shore of Lough Mask,
Tom O'Malley was educated at St Jarlath's College, Tuam,
and at University College Galway. He has taught as a
secondary teacher in Belfast and in Co. Meath.

A revised version of *Roots and Instincts*, the collection that
won the Patrick Kavanagh Poetry Award, was published in
1985 by Beaver Row Press as *By Lough Mask*. His most
recent collection, *Journey Backward* (Salmon Poetry 1998),
was awarded the 1998/9 Meath County Council/Tyrone
Guthrie Centre Regional Bursary Award. Tom O'Malley's
poems have appeared in numerous journals and anthologies,
including *Poetry Ireland Review, New Irish Writing, The Irish
Times, Mayo Anthology, Quarry and Lichen* (Canada) and
The Café Review (USA).

All the poems reprinted here, with the exception of 'Grief',
are from *Journey Backward*; 'Grief' appeared in both *Roots
and Instincts* and *By Lough Mask*.

Travelling Shop

That winter's night in the light of the shop
window, we helped, as usual, unload the van.
You had come back, tired, from your mountain run
and were busy counting your takings into the till.

We lifted out the unsold goods: the sugar
in brown paper bags, the cardboard boxes of tea,
cornflakes, custards, jellies, bread and jam
and then we tried our strength on the heavyweights.

We were never really short of sweets and biscuits:
your shelves were our orchard and forbidden fruit
found many ways to our jacket pockets; though
not without guilt – I wonder if you really knew.

That evening, I'll never know why, when our work
was done, you gave us two red apples each:
I locked mine in a biscuit tin for a week –
trying to preserve the gesture, not the fruit.

The Mallard

On the kitchen table under the harsh light
The wild-duck lies, a green sheen on its stiff neck;
The rust-webbed feet are crinkled, tense in death.
You said how you raised it from the shore at dusk
And lifted your metallic gun-barrel after it:
A harsh explosion belled your ear as the stock
Kicked and your spray of pellets outstripped its panic.
Now, the sharp eye is tight-lidded, that lemon beak
Is badly chipped; but yet as if it still wished
To hide beneath soft down that gross entrance which
Your pellets made, the stiff wing lies folded.

We are hunters, both. You with your rods, gun, traps
And bait express your nature, lore and prowess
But capture death. I must try in words to catch
That something most elusive your pellets missed
As wild and shy, the squawking mallard rose
Abruptly up from shore grass – to a grand, majestic
Flapping into twilight, its graceful neck outstretched
Its webbed feet flush with its smooth undercarriage.

Time-Share

Here, jagged grey limestone rock
is lashed by wintry waters
of Tom Kane's turlough –

a field of waves
he time-shares with
this Lough Mask wilderness.

For over half each year,
a wildlife habitat,
fishermen cast bait there;

but come mid-May
swans and wild-duck vacate
their winter tenancy

as brown-burnt mossy walls
and grass reappear
above shrunken waters.

The rest of the summer through
Tom's cattle graze
his fluctuant field.

Spring Cleaning

Often things have to get worse before getting better
as now, when you blur your side; I, mine.

You polish the windolene into the glass;
and I shine and shine until my blur is gone.

You point out some small imperfection, my side;
I point to a small speck on yours.

Again, we each shine away our observed blemishes
until at last one pane stands perfect between us.

Grief

With sharp, bright-edged spades,
Two diggers, aided by whiskey,
Cut a clean wound in the side
Of the world – six feet by three
By six – a sharp-edged cut,
Where boxed we laid you
Gently in; and stamped back
The dark flesh. For months
Sutured skin showed a wound
Unhealed. Each time I pass
I can still see the raised
Surgical scar and feel that
Clean, necessary wound they made
Slice by slice, deeper and deeper
With their sharp-edged spades.

Roots and Instincts

Grey-frigid, he stands out on a hard landscape
of streaked limestone, beside a glacial lake,
as stark as in some drawing by Edvard Munch.
He seems to lack all fruitful contact with rich soil,
tribal warmth or touch of a gentle god; and yet
he survives, absorbing sustenance like this ash
that persists, though stunted, in mysterious clefts
where no life is normally expected. I wonder at
the ingenuity of these roots, their prospecting instinct
that can suck up food from some secret source. What
brute will lives deep in both their natures
that can give them energy to live though warped – the ash
in its dwarfed ashness, he in his stark humanity.
And yet, both endure and somehow proclaim life
where white rock is chill even at high summer.

Garden Fire

I've stacked my garden fire
with old magazines, old newspapers.
Though the flames seem overpowered
they climb upwards round charred edges
leafing away each topmost page
which scrolls back inward on itself.

Methodically the orange flames
devour our yesterdays' stale news,
the glossy ads for motor cars,
the low-cut, high-fashion dresses;
models flaring now, as never before.

Yet sometimes leaving undigested
a weird residue of ashen negatives –
columns of tabloid trivia, headlines, ads
which I reread clearly as at first
in ghostly print still vivid as if unburnt.

In curious disbelief, I prod a page.
It stains my fingertips
with its grey ashes. I watch it crumble
under pressure into jigsaw flakes
which the spring-gusts catch
scattering their disjointed words
among apple trees and young fruit bushes.

1985

Roz Cowman was born in Cork in 1942 and
attended university there. Afterwards she taught in East and
West Africa for five years. Since returning to Ireland she has
worked mainly in adult education: in Waterford until 1989
and then in Cork where she still lives.

She first began writing poetry in 1976, receiving much
support from creative writing workshops given by Eavan
Boland, John Ennis and Michael Coady. Such workshops
were a rarity at that time and new writers found it difficult to
discover a forum where writing could be discussed or even
to learn the names of literary magazines. Roz Cowman's first
recognition came in 1982 when she received the Arlen
House Award and an Arts Council Bursary. *The Goose Herd*,
based on the collection that won the Patrick Kavanagh
Poetry Award, was published by Salmon Poetry in 1989. Her
later poetry has appeared in Irish, British and American
magazines and anthologies.

'Quadrille at the Duchess of Richmond's Ball' is published
here for the first time.

The Robber Bride

I amn't always my real self
with you but I had a great
time with you last night and you
not even here.

I was boiling the jam
all evening and the heat
and the street-children at their game
of being me –
the hotel's daughter –
'tis as good as Queenie Carrigaline
to hear them

Then it was eleven, and everyone gone
so a nice hot bath ... 'twas like blood
from the jam stains
I wished we could meet
only when I'd be clean
but sure that was only a dream
my love

Then in my room I was lonely
but I said I'd just rehearse
for you ... so I pictured you there
and I wore the silk pyjamas I told you about
in the pink and mauve
and then the plain pink silk
and then the nightie ... I asked you
how you liked them and you liked
the nightie best of all
I gave you a hug
and felt you'd want to hug me
with an etcetera

It was almost as good as
if you were there –
the hotel empty and the night
hot and red with the smell of jam

the whole top floor to myself
and I running from room
to room from mirror to mirror and
the pink and the mauve
and the silk

Annunciation

All day the sun has poured
its gases into the town
stone erodes   copper domes
liquefy   glare
makes terracotta faces
plate glass reverts
to silica

No shade the late traveller
will find no lapis dusk
to cushion his announcement
concrete heaves underfoot
clouds are significant
even the furniture's turned hostile

In what's left of air spermatozoa
float like pollen   she would gasp
for breath in the rush
of his descent beside her
but the atmosphere
vacuums to him

the frail tympani of her ears
snap like furze pods
and with everything still
unsaid between them
the word is made flesh

The Goose Herd

The first angels must have been
like this, intolerant, haughty,
slightly clumsy, their wings
more beautiful than themselves,

and not respectful to the godhead
but watching him, chins lifted,
hearing false notes with
spiritual ears.

There would have been no mutiny,
but a remembering of wild
blood at the equinox,
a stir of stony wings

against dark cloud, taking
the last light with them,
leaving the godhead resentful
because it missed their noisy blasphemies,

cursing them and naming as Hell
their destiny ... a wild, lonely place
of sudden laughs, wailings, grey
down clouding the sight like ash.

Meanings

a nice girl
of course and her family her
mother now was one of
and her father was be sure
to crack the boiled egg
sideways they'll have the
silver eggcups will burn
your hand so dont be saying
you want shop like
a landgrabber's child
but if tis shop remember
the country jam will run
through the holes

Longonot Crater Kenya 1968

We've gone beyond ourselves ...
let this be the aphelion
where air is thin, heat is half light and stinks
in fumaroles

No heroes on these march-lands
heroes need a crowd, a market,
songs. We have no breath
for song, and applause
is the rattle of Dead Sea fruit
on ash
What can we trade who scavenge
our humanity in this light
which is neither dog nor wolf

We should be glad to sleep
but something wild as a cat
lives here among the wormwood
and the ash
and hunts us down crooning
its memories of milk
and will not let us rest

The Kitchen Window

The Sunday mutton turns
in its pepper muslin
these June evenings.
Milk in the pantry breaks
into cirro-cumulus.
Talk pooters
between home and office
is lost in a backyard's dusk.

What lies beyond the glass hills
is chatoyancy and lures
like an old land
seen through a mullion.
You will not cross those hills again
now the equinox is done.

Caves eat the liver
of a sandstone hill where you watch
the flight of the photons
space-like separate
each
aware of the other.

Quadrille at the Duchess of Richmond's Ball

men's hands touch at the hub
of the *grande ronde*
under the gloves is bare
flesh that I never touch and sinew
against bone and muscle and the push
of blood

after this ball they will be
together four on four
gloves off
pulses pulling bare
hand to hand

while my pulse drips life
into the maw of that white bitch
whose sucking orbit mocks me
in this ladies' *ronde* that orbits

flesh of young men held
by each other like on like
gloves off
in their dream of blood

1986

Padraig Rooney was born in Monaghan and
educated at St Macartan's College, at Maynooth University
and at the Sorbonne.

His early stories were published in the *Irish Press* 'New Irish
Writing' page, and in *Best Irish Short Stories 2 & 3* (Paul
Elek), all edited by David Marcus. He has published one
novel, *Oasis* (Poolbeg) and one collection of poems, *In the
Bonsai Garden* (Raven Arts Press) and received two Arts
Council Bursaries. Recent poems have appeared in *Scanning
the Century: The Penguin Book of Poetry in the Twentieth
Century*, edited by Peter Forbes, in *The Backyards of Heaven*,
edited by John Ennis and Stephanie McKenzie, and in
magazines.

He has lived and taught abroad for many years and is
currently Head of English at Basel International School
in Switzerland.

His Winter Laboratory

My father lived in winter laboratories,
unheated, where future experiments were stored.
The upper rooms of a Catholic seminary
held trays of cold birds' eggs, precious mercury.
He knew his natural science by heart,
the properties of stones, the laws which defied
the law of gravity, a fulcrum's breaking point.
His brain was a fertile hatchery.

Radium glowed in a special room beyond my reach,
scalpels for dissection in their velvet drawers.
His leather apron hung behind the door,
grey and flaccid, reeking of the tannery.
What failed discoveries hovered in the ether
which always stained his hands, I'll never know.
Caustic marks, lingering stigmata of an art
that moved and classified like a perfect surgeon.

The parts of animals, a chart of nature's tree
shone in snowy light above the bunsen burners.
An anatomy detailed, all its articulations known.
His oven burned with the light of science,
atomic clay mined from far-flung quarries
he shaped to molecules hard and round as marbles.
Those home-made mobiles revolved in outer space,
clear and cold, his clockwork constellations.

The Whirligig Dream

i

On my first night back in the mango republic
you showed me the anatomy theatre in the dark.

Then we went back to your place and made love
under a poster of a skeleton from Hoffmann-La Roche,

all two hundred and six bones laid out and tagged
in Latin and English. Post-coital and jet-lagged,

I retold my story of wild parties with the sons
of those Basel drug barons, when I was sixteen.

After military service they drank champagne
from the barrels of their Swiss army guns.

Now I slept in arms smelling of formalin
and woke to bones littering the counterpane,

fibula, tibia, assorted ribs, a hand
reticulated like Meccano, your take-home hoard

from gross anatomy. We played knucklebones
over breakfast with some poor Yorick's knuckles

and made love again like the old times, quick,
before hitting the streets of the mango republic.

ii

Ten years of my life in this capital of sleaze,
boomtown of the East, one of the emerging democracies.

When you were small I had a recurring dream
I called the whirligig dream (my child's name

for helicopter). Returning on a rescue mission,
I hung from a rope ladder like Action Man

while you were below within arm's reach
as we lifted and whirled, making that final pitch

for freedom across the roof-top heliport.
Whether you made it or didn't make it

into the wind machine's decisive take,
I woke up sweating in the tropical dark

and called you before you went to school.
When the army opened fire outside the Royal Hotel

on the demonstrators for democracy,
among the fifty-three dead was a boy

your age, blown away under a flame tree,
while I sat at home and watched it on BBC.

Proust's Day

Some days I don't wake until night.
I summon the servants with a bell:
shaving water, stale newspapers,
café au lait piping hot, lots of it,
and croissant crumbs on the quilt.
By midnight my day takes shape
from a little light reverie, a puzzle,
the thousand pieces of a masterpiece.
I hear the church bells ring the hours,
the aerial bombardments, the all-clear.
The servants tiptoe as Mama told them
long ago, leaving trays at my door.
I might summon a sealed carriage
and ride around the dark boulevards,
pick up the scum of the aerodromes.
The squares are empty at that hour,
the men mute. I get them to talk dirty
over my pack of snaps, a royal flush
of Duchesses and Contessas, Mama
among them. I pay the butcher boys
to bring me fat rats from the abattoir,
to stick them with hatpins, beat them
round my cork-lined walls as I watch.
Once they killed a chicken as I came.
I order in *purée* and champagne,
a chamber orchestra to play Fauré,
note their eyes, their lips, the curl
of their jumped-up moustaches.
I'm in bed by nine, correcting proofs
by electric light, the shutters closed.

Pool

There's always a pool parlour wherever one goes
(think I'll use this line in a poem) if one gets bored.
Elizabeth Bishop, *Letters*

There's always a pool parlour wherever one goes.
I travel light, with a two-bit screw-together cue
in this customized case, my monogram worked
into the Italian leather. I looked like a hitman,
or woman, in the old days, stepping off the trains
into a scuzzy underworld where I'd play pool,

professionally, for money – in those station pool
parlours cum barbershops where the Mafia goes.
I'd chat up hoods in the smokers of the trains –
faggot amateur, they'd think, fingering my screwy cue,
but time and again they fell for it to a man.
My smooth-faced con trick always worked.

In these Med towns the men are over-worked
or on the dole. Either way they're game for pool.
I loved the crack of the break, the man-to-man
lickety-split of the shoeshine boy as he goes
about his blow-job in the john, the tick of the cue
in smoke-blue parlours underneath the trains.

Ah, those runaway cross-dressers riding the trains
with stiletto hearts and false eyelashes. They'd worked
nights since they were boys and could come right on cue!
On bank holiday weekends we'd celebrate and pool
our stakes, live it up in Naples or in Rome. Money goes
quickly with low-life Romeos. I took it like a woman,

but where it mattered I potted them like a man,
one by one under the arriving and departing trains,
the reds, the yellows, the blues. Luck comes and goes
but with me it's skill in adversity that's always worked,
the hormone rush that comes with beating men at pool
I've had since I was twelve, and chalked my first cue.

My Scrabble dictionary says it's a variation of *queue*.
You wouldn't care to play to pass the time, young man?
I'm a dab hand at Scrabble, but nothing like I am at pool,
and we've hours to kill before we board our trains.
Truth is, my con-man tricks haven't really worked
in these *termini* for years. Youth too comes and goes,

like a cue-ball potting back and forth in sixteen goes.
I'm worked to death these days picking up a man,
and a spot of pool might do the trick until our trains.

The Disappearing Act

A wanted ad in *Conjurers Magazine* in 1906:
boy assistant for carney hall artiste. Brooklyn area.

Regular conjuring work was scarce then, before the Great War.
Auditions took place upstairs in a dime hall cum stripper club

called *Now You See It, Now You Don't*. His stage name was de Kolta
and all down the coast we pulled the punters with a ouija board,

did card tricks, escapes, disappearing acts: one called Pandora
a classic of its kind that sent the audience psychotic.

Boxes locked inside coffins inside trunks, while de Kolta
released the trap door, waved his wand and made me disappear.

A tense silence. I held my last breath. He clicked finger and thumb.
Ninety years ago, mister, since he said abracadabra.

1987

Anthony Glavin was born in 1945 in Dublin, where
he now teaches in the Royal Irish Academy of Music.

'Born Losers' is from *The Wrong Side of the Alps* (The
Gallery Press 1989), based on the collection that won the
Patrick Kavanagh Poetry Award. This volume was short-listed
for both the Irish Times/Aer Lingus Poetry Prize and an Irish
Book Award. He received a major Arts Council Bursary in
1990. The nine poems from a new work-in-progress are
published for the first time here.

Born Losers

*There is no fate that cannot
be surmounted by scorn.*
– Albert Camus

I

When the days go badly wrong,
Why is it *Never again!* we cry,
As though by harping on that old song
We'd change, or discover why,

Stuck in its lousy refrain,
We let things happen the way they do –
The quarrels, the awkwardness, the pain,
The being unwilling to continue ...

And putting it right! Such a fuss
Hardly seems worth it in the end,
For tomorrow unfolds to the self-same mess,
And if we slacken and pretend

What happens must be good enough,
Since we can cope, and not despair
At the way the love and joy and stuff
We fear, others dare,

There lurks an unsleeping sense
Of happiness missed-out on before we die –
Happiness perhaps not given a chance –
No way, no how, no why.

II

You can't avoid 'em, once in a while –
Pinch-lipped, sloth-eyed, their grudged-out voices
Sickened by life. Born losers. They've had their choices.
'How goes it?' you ask, and they smile

Aggrievedly, as though they might mean
To heal themselves, only it's too far gone now –
'One copes. One's got at least to learn to live with how
Unliveable with it's been …'

Which means, of course, without love,
As though they'd managed to weigh and found it wanting –
'Ah yes, that splendid disaffection of the young …'
Difficult not to laugh,

But to have to nod and sit and listen
As they agonize, in a welter of grim self-loathing,
Over what in the end will anyway about amount to nothing –
Impossible. Dear heart, compassion

Is a reserved discretion of the mind
That pity, like boredom, deadens as it infects.
Who'd want to sicken of what a feigned disinterest lacks?
No hard feelings, you understand,

But next time some misery-freak intones
'I am the man! I bled! I suffered! I was there!'
'Jesus wept!' I'll snarl, 'Do I have to bloody care?
– Go 'phone *that* in to the Samaritans!'

Nine Poems from a Work-in-Progress

RALLY

Mile-high light-beams slicing into the sky.
A cathedral of ice.

His use of the pronoun 'we'
As though belonging to the same species.

IN THE MOUNTAINS

On the Terrace with the Führer. Wonderfully relaxed
And liberated. I am so thankful and happy

To hear him enthuse about the great, great future.
The sun has broken through again. Hitler-weather.

MENGELE

A death-smile as he calms and then injects them –
Phenol, or that terrible bubble of air –

His eyes unseeing, lifeless – how easily lost souls become
A habit of appearing to but not being there –

A ROOF-SLIDE OPENS, A ROOF-SLIDE CLOSES

Hiss of cyanide displacing air.
Headache-pulse of fists on a locked steel door.

Belching of a cremation-detail slugging beer.
Ash-whispers off an angled shovel. There. There.

NEAR WEIMAR 1944

Sometimes we wonder about the factories –
Evenings the wind is wrong and the lindens toss

A drizzle of soot and ash all over the magnolias,
We cannot meet each other's eyes.

ANOTHER TATOO FOR FRAU KOCH

She would have them garrotted, cleanly, then
Flayed, cured, stretched, cut, sewn.

You climbed to her attic for a private view.
Lampskins. Shadow-traffic. What can I say?

ENTER, FLEEING

One unfortunate –
Tottering, skeletal, a sideshow-cripple-on-stilts –

Drew himself up when he saw Eisenhower's stripes
And tried to salute.

AT THE WARSAW GHETTO MEMORIAL

Willy Brandt fell
To his knees, head bowed –

'I simply did
What people do when words fail.'

A CIVILIZATION

Dark opening – this way, that way –
ARBEIT MACHT FREI

(*works free*)
Unnatural selections – where silence – it all to say.

1988

Angela Greene was born in England but her family
moved to Dublin when she was very young. She was
educated at the Dominican College, Eccles Street and
trained as a nurse at the Mater Hospital. She was always
interested in painting and literature but it was only in the
eighties, after her four children were reared, that she
started writing seriously.

She was a prizewinner in the Bloodaxe Books National
Poetry Competition in 1987 and was a runner-up in the
Hennessey/Sunday Tribune Literary Award in 1988. A
selection of her poems appeared in *Trio Poetry 6* in 1990
and her collection *Silence and the Blue Night*, from which
the poems in this anthology are taken, was published by
Salmon Poetry in 1993. Her poems have been read on RTÉ
and BBC radio and performed in *Sunny Side Plucked* at
Project Arts Centre, Dublin.

Angela Greene's premature death in February 1997 was a
sad loss to Irish poetry.

Silence and the Blue Night

Here is the place
you would want to arrive at
after a long journey preceded
by grief and much delay.
There is a brown mountain.
Lavender clouds roof a sea
so wide and level the image
blanks the mind. Night is falling.
From the terrace you see a farmhouse
with ochred arches lit
from within. Its beasts are settled,
folded into rest. It is a scene
of domestic tenderness
offering its warmth.

But
it is too artful a backdrop
for the mother
calling anxiously to her child.
He has wandered off
beyond the rocks to the sea
leaving his blue bag spilling
its contents over the red tiles.
She calls his pet name, twice,
but the third call becomes
a frail and exotic sound –
some primitive bird's perhaps?

She risks the rough ground, mind
racing, she is
already elsewhere her torchlight
a flame plunging through lakes
of blue air. Now the clouds are
deeper purple, agitating darkly
to loose and grab at the moon.
In hot dust, among dry stones,
she stumbles; lizards
crackle in the scrub. The rocks

are full of shadows. The sea is a
hiss on distant shingle.

Again she calls but her cry
falls in thin and difficult
echoes and is absorbed
into the mountain. Is the name
really a name, or a memory
unravelling inside her skull?
Is she calling her child
or is she
the child being called?
She has forgotten where she is.

She stands.
Night deepens, merciless.
The lit farmhouse, the terrace
with its globe of light
are out of reach now. Like ships
becalmed on a sea of dark,
they are remote, inhuman. She dips
the torchbeam. Around her
the indigo stillness glooms.
Silence and the blue night
engulf the boy
whose pale limbs she is desperate
to arrange in sleep.

Letting Go

The false security
of the simple
and the ordinary.

I lift the latch, push,
take several steps
across the bright linoleum
toward the dresser shouting,
'Kids, kids, I can hardly hear my ears,'
when I realize I am in a dream.

The fool in me
not wanting to accept change.

In that moment I had my children
as I still want them to be. Kilts
and knee-socks, short pants
and t-shirts. The soft splash
as milk
falls from the tray of the high chair.
I'm reaching back to them
from chat through chores
to play. What I didn't know then …
That rowdy kitchen was a piece
of cake. I ruled the roost.

Now these young men and women
sprawl over so much space
they scare me. The world's
the oyster their minds
prise wide. They talk
inches above my head. Their
laughter and their language leap
beyond me.   Now

I am forced to look at time
in another way. Not
as so many grains of sand

flowing from glass belly
to glass belly, but how,
through the persistent gnawing
of years, I've weathered
as I watch them grow. And
how at last, as I let go
and slip behind them, I ease
my bones into the universe.

Terrorist's Wife

A phone-call takes him
into the dark for weeks.
In the mornings, his absence
fills me with dread. I thin my eyes
to watch for cars that come to wait
down in the street. All day
I move from room to room. I polish
each spotless place
to a chill shining. Fear tracks me
like hunger. In the silence,
the walls grow wafer-thin.
The neighbours wear masks –
tight lips, veiled looks, such
fine tissues of knowing.
My mother doesn't visit. I drag
my shopping from the next town.

Once, putting his clean shirts away,
my dry hands touched a shape
that lay cold and hard. I wept then,
and walked for hours in the park.
I listened for his name in the news.
When I looked at our sleeping son
my sadness thickened.
His comings are like his goings –
a swift movement in the night.

At times, he can sit here for days
meticulously groomed; primed,
watching soccer games on TV,
our child playful on his lap.
But scratch the smooth surface
of his mood, and how
the breached defences spit their fire.

Now, when he holds me to him,
I know I taste murder
on his mouth. And in the darkness,
when he turns from me, I watch him
light a cigarette. In his palm
the lighter clicks and flames.
Balanced, incendiary.

1989

Pat Boran was born in Portlaoise in 1963 and
currently lives in Dublin, where he has been a writer-in-
residence with Dublin City Libraries, Dublin Corporation and
Dublin City University, and programme director of the Dublin
Writers' Festival.

His four collections are *The Unwound Clock* (which won the
Patrick Kavanagh Poetry Award), *Familiar Things* (1993), *The
Shape of Water* (1996), *As the Hand, the Glove* (2001), all
published by The Dedalus Press. A *New and Selected
Poems* is due out in the UK in 2004. As well as his own
poems, he has also published translations of Jean Orizet and
Álex Susanna, both with Dedalus. His first fiction work for
children, *All the Way from China* (Poolbeg 1998), was short-
listed for the Bisto Award. Among his non-fiction titles are
The Portable Creative Writing Workshop (Salmon Poetry
1999) and *A Short History of Dublin* (Marino Books 2000).
Co-editor (with Peter Sirr) of the *Dublin Fifteen: Poems of
the City* CD anthology, he has also edited *Poetry Ireland
Review* and *PORTAL*, Ireland's literature and arts journal for
EXPO2000. As well as contributing to a number of radio and
TV arts shows, he has presented the RTÉ television books
programme *Undercover* and the RTÉ Radio 1 poetry
programme *The Enchanted Way*.

The first poem here is from *The Unwound Clock*.

House

Water clanks from the tap
like a chain – a lifetime

since anything has moved here
but rats and birds. I see

the last inhabitants as a father
and son, the father

sending the son off to the city
with a handshake and a pocket

of old pound notes.
He might as well be sending him

to bring home the time
without a watch to carry it.

Children

Children in ill-fitting uniforms
drive adults to school, and children
argue the cost of tobacco
in the Newsagent's nearby.

You must have noticed them.

And in the mornings they rise to slaughter pigs,
cook breakfast, solve crosswords at the office …
Or they send tiny adults into minefields,
barefoot, with pictures
of Khomeini around their necks,
their old toes searching the sand
for death.

And children queue for Bingo
on Ormond Quay, on Mary Street,
and douse their leaking take-aways with vinegar.

And children talk and smoke incessantly
in Eastern Health Board waiting-rooms,
always moving one seat to the right,
someone's parents squabbling over trinkets
on the worn linoleum.

And it is always children
who will swear for their tobacco – children
with beards and varicose veins –
and children, dressed as policemen,
who pull their first corpses from the river.

And who is it who makes love in the dark
or in the light, who haunts
and who does all our dying for us,
if not children?

We leave their fingerprints
on everything we touch.

A Natural History of Armed Conflict

The wood of the yew
made the bow. And the arrow.
And the grave-side shade.

Still Life with Carrots

When I discover a carrot, like this one
grown old, forgotten on a shelf
behind bottles of oil, herbs and spices,
all those *nouveaux arrivées*, I feel myself

drawn to it. It's as if all
the wonderful meals my life has been made of,
the exotic tables at which I have sat,
had never existed, as if during love –

making a former lover had come
into my mind, or a neighbour, long dead
had knocked on the door and let himself in,
as of old, trailing the earth from his grave.

The politeness accosts me. Almost as frail
as my father in his hospital bed
those last long months, this carrot seems
to have something to tell me. The fact is, in the end,

the formidable weakens, the once proud
become stooped and sad. The lost
no longer recognize themselves.
And so it goes for all our vegetable loves:

the pea dries up; the tomato weeps
and weeps an ectoplasmic mess;
lettuce browns like an old book;
potatoes send up flares of distress;

but carrots just age there, waiting to be found,
as the plates on the table, like the planets, go around.

Neighbours

They were the ones we told jokes about,
the red-necked, spud-thick family up the road:
how she smashed the car into the gate
going for her driving test, how once the door
came away in the father's hand like a sheet

of old wallpaper. And then their kid.
Helping daddy one day paint the fence
around their concrete garden, he knocked the tin
then ran away in tears, his yellow footprints
and their yellow footprints all over the street

like a dance-step map. Wee Johnny,
which is what they called him, never seemed
quite right after that. The poor wee mon, he
was frightened of his shadow. At Halloween,
kids knocked on their door and threw him money

to see if he'd cry. Which he always did.
In school they ganged up on him in the yard
and made him sing *The Sash*. More than once he peed
his pants. More than once his furious dad
had to come and take him home at speed.

When the sister married, true to form
the old man drank so much he fell face first
into the wedding cake. The honeymoon,
in Ballyshannon, was a total farce.
The groom met an old flame and he was gone.

Their flat-faced dog liked to chase parked cars.
The mother opened doors in her dressing gown.
We laughed till we were sick, and then we laughed
even more. The day before they finally left town,
the kid came second in a boxing match.

1990

Sinéad Morrissey was born in Northern Ireland in
1972 and educated in Belfast and at Trinity College Dublin.
She spent four years living in Japan and New Zealand
before settling in Belfast. She has been writer-in-
residence at the Royal Festival Hall and at Queen's
University.

She has published two collections with Carcanet Press:
There Was Fire in Vancouver (1996) and *Between Here and
There* (2002). She has won an Eric Gregory Award (1996),
the Rupert and Eithne Strong Award (2002), the MacCaulay
Fellowship from the Arts Council of Ireland (2002), and has
been short-listed for the T.S. Eliot Prize (2002).

The first poem here is from the unpublished collection that
won her the Patrick Kavanagh Poetry Award; the others are
from a forthcoming collection, *The State of the Prisons*.

The Cave Hill in February

This is where men in macs come, out on a limb
And drenched by rain. Remembered climbs from childhood
And my grandmother's warnings of bad men and motorbikes
Settle in footholds and off-the-track ditches.
I imagine the silence is appalled at something.
My thoughts have hushed here.

Out at the top, everything is exposed to a wind
That sweeps me clean and whole again.
A chasm, open for dissection, is telling me its secrets
And the sea is riddled. The sun ignites the docks –
Going down on industrial cranes. A ship
Is swallowed at the end of my sight.
Nobody comes.

I walk the mile downhill, resting halfway
On a solitary log that lost its family in the falling.
Someone is discovering a tree house in the forest
That scales the side of the hill;
Sometimes the air brings me another one's voice;
Somewhere in the sprawling, shrunken city
A gun is going off and a door is being shut on a life.

Migraine

It wasn't long before my vision blurred.
The shock. The chocolate. The thirst.
Eight hours in. The leader's face went slack
from the left side, as though his cheekbone cracked
and slithered free of him, weeping gunshot.
Then a tangle of darkness like a Rorschach blot
where his expression had been, opening inward …
I knew what it was once the starlight started.
Not liberation – no special forces falling from the ceiling.
This was my cross, my cleansing,
my monthly reckoning,
my migraine time rolled round
again to take me over and close me down.
The piled explosives by the fifteenth aisle
looked eaten with flame, but shimmeringly so, while
dying fires pulsed off and on along the stage,
as though the threads of things had frayed
to let the light through. My awful light. Light in the wrong place.
Like the sun at midnight or blood on the moon's face.
Eleven when it first descended. Had I gone blind
to see the whole world punctured from behind?
Pain was payment afterwards. It fell in blows –
planes hitting runways, slapstick pianos
crashing down stairs or hurtling out of windows.
I learned to turn to the wall, to strain to be empty,
to be animal and insular in sickness, to ossify,
to reckon blessings on my fingers as I wept.
The half who were women were padded and desperate.
Their voices were slick with contempt for the hostages
and lust for an ending that would splatter their message
from the newsstands of Moscow to the gun slums of Washington.
Their faces were veiled in black. Their hurt souls shone.
There is a war, they said, *somewhere off the map from where we are,
and we will bring it to you.* Horror poured out in a glittering theatre,
and held there. Act II. They stormed the stage yelling
Allahu Akbar. And now I was blinded by lightning
while my head was filling with blood like a black pudding.
I came for the stage effects: the bomber

from the war of my grandfather
falling out of the sky. The revolution glimpsed through fire and ash.
The love interest. Songs to sing in the bath,
afterwards. We were fed confectionary from the interval kiosk
which made my body bloom. Water was scarce.
Talk was policed
Russia's first musical had its throat sliced.

Driving Alone on a Snowy Evening

There is no reason that I know
to go on waking, eating, so
I turn the urgent wipers off
and watch the screen sift up with snow.

They'll conjure emptiness, despair,
disease in the wings, a failed career,
those inward, ticking moments when
the seduction of stopping obliterates fear.

The car purrs on. I do not brake.
The choice of crash I leave to fate –
a tree, a bridge, a railway line.
Behind the brightness dark shapes wait.

The snow and ceiling kiss, then meet.
The view's as white as a winding sheet.
The heart still beats *repeat, repeat*.
The heart still beats *repeat, repeat*.

Genetics

My father's in my fingers, but my mother's in my palms.
I lift them up and look at them with pleasure –
I know my parents made me by my hands.

They may have been repelled to separate lands,
to separate hemispheres, may sleep with other lovers –
but in me they touch where fingers link to palms.

With nothing left of their togetherness but friends,
who quarry for their image by a river,
at least I know their marriage by my hands.

I shape a chapel where a steeple stands.
And when I turn it over,
my father's by my fingers, my mother's by my palms

demure before a priest reciting psalms.
My body is their marriage register.
I re-enact their wedding with my hands.

So take me with you, take up the skin's demands
for mirroring in bodies of the future.
I'll bequeath my fingers, if you bequeath your palms.
We know our parents make us by our hands.

From *The State of the Prisons: A History of John Howard, Prison Reformer, 1726–1790*

I

I am a stranger and a pilgrim here.
I burn my letters, decline a monument, take heart
from the body's incontinence. The spirit departs.
The field hospitals of Russia with their horrendous dead
must carry me home to the Lord my Maker
where all my fathers' fathers stand assembled.

I see these soldiers' faces when I sleep.
And then they cloud and clear again as the child's
who stopped me on the road to ask the time
and tried to steal my watch. How sick she is.
And then she splits, becomes three women beating hemp
in a bridewell, missing eyelids.

Death has no terrors for me.
I have ridden the devil's coach-road, I have discovered
it leads, in every city in Europe, to the mansions of governors ...
Powders fizz in a glass. The admiral who has travelled
thirty miles to smile encouragingly
tries to change the subject but his voice unravels.

Death sits in my frame. And death shall have dominion
where all bodies are. 70,000 Russian soldiers died the year before
I washed up on the far shore of the Crimea.
This figure summoned me to Stepanovka –
a detour from my quest to find the origin
of plague. Now all such quests are over.

There is a village where a river flows
through a grove of pine trees. It is peaceful and obscure,
called Dauphigny. A Frenchman I befriended came from there.
We passed it on our journey south.
Bury me here in my chapel clothes
and let my body face the river mouth.

Fame saddens heaven. Suffer no stone to be raised to me,
nor details of my life and works be given at the gravebed,
nor mourners come. Erect a sundial over my head
instead of an inscription. Read from the psalms
of beholding His face in righteousness. Forget me. To posterity,
I leave a syphilitic son, and a vision of prisons.

1991

Sheila O'Hagan grew up in Dublin and moved to
London when she was nineteen. In 1989 she returned to live
in Dublin. She began writing poetry in 1988 and has
published two collections, *The Peacock's Eye* (Salmon Poetry
1992) and *The Troubled House* (Salmon Poetry/Poolbeg
1995). She is currently working on a third volume of poems
and a collection of short stories.

Among the awards she has won for her poetry are the
Goldsmith Prize (1988); the Hennessey/Sunday Tribune
Award for New Poet of the Year (1993), five awards from
Listowel Writers' Week and in 2000 the Strokestown
International Poetry Award for a single poem. In 1994 she
was writer-in-residence for Co. Kildare and edited *Under
Brigid's Cloak*, an anthology of Kildare writers. Sheila
O'Hagan has conducted numerous poetry workshops,
including one for prisoners in Wormwood Scrubs Prison,
and has also run a Radio 9 FM poetry competition for Irish
prisoners. She has just completed three years as guest
editor of the *Cork Literary Review*.

'Elegy for Mark' won the European Year of Solidarity for
Women Prize in 1996.

Photo credit: Steve Humphreys

Mozart's Kitchen

They flow over you that winter day,
the quartets for the King of Prussia,
notes crowding in the cat's dish,
spilling beneath the table
where you hide, avoiding God
who sends you a continuous
rumpus in the head,
counterpoint of children's cries,
drumbark of scrunty dog,
wind plucking at the housecracks –
harmonic twists feathering away
into a slow poem.

The stove is cold,
your starling has just died,
(Constanze is away in Baden Baden).
In the corner stands the little maid
who teaches you silence.
Yesterday you kissed her
and the still place in your soul
arched like a clef. Listen, you whispered,
listen to the spit of rain
counting itself on the window-pane.

Today is cold, outside
the city is an orchestra of sound,
Constanze dearest wife is home
(the little maid has gone).
A candle gutters, shadows
of minims, breves, crochets
are thrown onto the wall,
something holy and unwell
follows you to your sickbed.
Leaning to write it down
you slip into the dark
to finish your own requiem.

September The Fourth
Elegy For Ted

At four am today my lover died.
He didn't reach for me or call my name
Dreaming he would waken by my side
But turned his face and shuddered as some shame
Or haunting shook him and his mouth gave cry
To a portentous and unearthly pain.

Between darkness and dawn that cry of pain
And nothing warm has touched me since it died.
An ethos of cold starlight I can't name
Possessed my love while he lay by my side,
Something strange, unhuman, born of shame.
He had not said goodbye, called out or cried.

Some ghost or spirit left his mouth that cried
Out and he'd gone from me, had gone in pain
Into an alien world yet as he died
He drew my spirit to him, gave her my name.
Something possessed him as he left my side,
His face was turned away as though in shame.

I cupped his absent face and murmured shame
To that which claimed him for my love had cried
As though some shady trafficking in pain,
some curse or Judas kiss by which he died
Unknowingly in another's name,
Had come to term as he lay down beside

The one he loved. Perhaps lying by his side
Fearful in sleep, I had called up that shame
And he, my love, unknowingly had cried
Out in redemption for another's pain
As though a chosen victim. My love died
Because some cursed spirit took his name

For he was loved and honoured in his name
And I, as I lay sleeping by his side
Guarding his innocence, knew of no shame.
On the stark cusp of dusk and dawn he cried
Aloud so strange my heart burned cold with pain.
Not one warm thought has touched me since he died.

Still I call his name. All hope has died.
My unspent love's my pain. I have not cried.
Such is winter's shame, all's bare outside.

The Return of Odysseus to Ithaca

When he limped home smelling of the world, stood under
The great gate of the courtyard, shreds of vigour
In the wiry hair, the ageing limbs still sinewed,
She saw him from her window, knew she'd acted right
But hard with anger for the loveless wait, withdrew
Into the shadows of her room, for three days cried
To her unborn sons, counted twenty notches
On the olive post he'd hewn and whittled for their bed,
Heard his bellowed rage from the old banquet hall
Where her suitors preyed, swagger of the warrior
His dander up, cudgelled skulls, blood on the tapestries,
And when his anger spent, he leant exhausted by the fireplace
She fixed her face and hair, came down to him, cradled
His fading manhood and drew the sting of their lost years.

The Troubled House

The purpose of poetry is to remind us how difficult it is
to remain just one person, for our house is open, there
are no keys in the doors, and invisible guests come in
and out at will.
Czeslaw Milosz

I live in a troubled house,
walk backwards, stumble over things,
a piano tinkers, the fretting wind
cannot find a tune, eyes dark as anemones
follow me from room to room.
Along the corridor, shuffle of empty shoes,
petitioners, their hands held out for love.

My dears, you cannot live with me,
the moment's passed, having no breath
you exhale loss. Besides it is my guilt
excites you, another country where you died.
I want to say to you, yes, come tonight
from three to four, I'll leave the door ajar
but do not stay. Let silence settle
like an old dog on the floor. This house
must decompose. At daybreak
I'll close it down, go into the garden,
wait for snow to spread in absolution.

Mirage

When the boy appeared out there
Pale as the haze of noon,
All wrapped in shimmering linen,
His arms in flames, his eyes
Full of his own being,

It was a visitation unheralded
That found me drowsy under
Summer trees, the air so bright,
The boy so stilled, so shined,
Wearing his ineffable peace.

Yet even as I fathomed him
His fading linen snooked
On the wind, the sun withdrew,
The earth shook itself and I
Was left with rounded eyes

To shiver in the grass,
Feel the waning day,
See the stilly hole
Of light in the shaded tree
Where a god had been.

Elegy For Mark

In the stored past of an attic
I, a woman growing old
Hold a coat, Oxfam, with rabbit pin
That shapes the lie of your presence
Arrange the sleeves in an embrace
Search for a familiar hair, a stain
Mourning as older women do
The bodies of the young.

Watch how your shade invades the pool
Of sun the window has let in
Hear the purr of the Silver Dream
Racer along a country road
See it turn treacherous
As you bend to the fatal spin,
The reflection of your stillness
In the still turning wheels.

I, a woman growing old
Perform a ritual for another's son
Loved as my own, rock myself
Into a grief black as the coat
I hold lest you be there, once a year
Climbing the height of this house
Far from any who might hear
The beat of the heart mending.

Angel Preening

for Kosova

Back from Earth, still thrusting itself
up to her in all its filth, she perches

On that cloud with a rosy tint
to the left, furiously preening,

One wing across a knee as she licks
the muck between her plumes, worries

The stains of the foul rivers' beds,
her face moody with secrets. Driven thus

To recover her radiance, she tuts
and fumes, the task almost beyond her.

Soon she will shake herself, take off
for the shining unseenness of home,

Leaving below the cries,
the bloodbaths, of the slain,

Her small feet clean, her body glow
fusing with that Delphinian blaze.

1992

Áine Miller was born in Cork city and attended
University College Cork. She lived for many years in London
and Surrey before settling in Dublin with her husband and
children. Her first poetry collection, *Goldfish in a Baby Bath*
(Salmon Poetry 1994), includes the poems for which she
won the Patrick Kavanagh Poetry Award. In 1998 she
graduated from the new MPhil in Creative Writing at Trinity
College Dublin and her second collection, *Touchwood*
(Salmon 2000), includes poems presented for that degree.

Among the numerous awards she has won for her poetry
and short stories are: a Hennessey/Sunday Tribune Award;
the Kilkenny Prize for fiction, 1992; the Moore Medallion for
fiction in 1994 and for poetry in 1995; the Gerard Manley
Hopkins prize; the Maria Edgeworth Prize; the Boyle Festival
Poetry Prize; the Book Stop New Writers Prize; and the
William Allingham Prize. Her poems are included in volume V
of *The Field Day Anthology of Irish Writing*, *Six for Gold*,
Jumping off Shadows (Cork University Press) and *The White
Page* (Salmon).

The first poem here, 'Seventeen', is from the collection that
won the Patrick Kavanagh Poetry Award; the others are all
from *Touchwood*.

Seventeen

I had on a terrible frock,
red check that rustled, my hair in a bang,
a brooch shaped like a poodle dog,

even so at that social you sang
Granada in my ear only, taught me
to the tune of Jealousy the tango,

though when we walked across the City,
the two of us in my swagger coat,
arms twined, we lumbered clumsily

as three-legged runners, quoting
Spanish poems as our touching pulses beat
Latin rhythms, the secrets told

more for lovers than for such as me
and you, yet every bit as binding, more,
they're still unspoken, but when we

kissed across the bicycle at my door,
shy as seedlings forced into the light,
we butted noses like a pair of Eskimos,

you muttered gruff goodbyes, took flight
down Summerhill, with borrowed bike and clips,
for one whole minute in the light

of dining-room mirror, my lips
grazed by the hair of your unshaven chin,
were wide awake, beautiful.

In His Eye

We have him all to ourselves,
the clutch of us, in the Bedford
on Sunday. Rain. The van

bucking the sea wall, us
on the watch for a break
in the clouds, one ray

on Ringabella sands,
for the *Into yeer togs*,
and the *Get yeerselves wet*,

that'll earn us wafers
from Peig's. We are off out,
dainty as goats on the stones

       at Fountainstown, turning
       to wave at him, dark,
       still at the wheel, sure

       we alone have the eye of him
       now, scamper and squeal
       in the froth of the breakers,

       Signs of the Cross, and brave
       for a splash, till damp
       at the crotch our costumes

       flood into colour. Pictures
       from Magic Painting books,
       we are shining and streaming

       like flowers in the first
       rainy morning, their cups
       turned to the source. Asleep

in his seat, he is cross
when he's roused. We take turns
with the towel behind him,

peel off, kick ourselves
free of those colours
of loving, screwed now

into twists like the salt
always there in the heel of
Smith's crisps he throws us

at Cogan's. We wait in the van,
an edge on our tongues,
and nothing ever enough.

Man-Child

She who first felt him slither on her chest
after the whoosh of birth,
wondered at his balled-up fists
and his foamy aghast mouth.

Before his gums would clamp upon her breast
she had to pinch his cheeks,
press her thumb to the hollow
in his chin, prise apart lips.

Reluctant suckler. Who was more distressed?
She who longed to pour out
love as sweetmilk on his rage,
swollen with the weight of it.

He turning marble in that baby nest
sooner than allow some
other resource than himself
was needed for survival.

Twelve years on, even love becomes abscessed.
She recoils from his fang,
in her old silted wells, sure
he is about his business.

Adam

Evening. The sheep are restless,
tack in circles, follow shadows
to their bitter edges, tentatively,
out onto unpromising lands.
There's a new smell in the air,
hot, sticky, the colour of a horn
played loud, louder, loudest,

the colour behind his eyes.
New segments in his head are
full to bursting with the blare,
angry voices and the sullen
clouded face of his eldest son.
What he fears most he hasn't
a name for. He searched all day.

Now his eye is caught by
fidgeting sheep, by another dark
in their midst. He calls a name,
races to where his son sleeps,
tries to rouse him, cradling
his head. *How cold against*
my cheek. How his head lolls.

Abel. Abel. This is no sleep.
In this nightmare bundling –
eyes lips stiffening limbs
fumy skin veins clotted curls
the newest orifice bleeding –
a word presses to be born.
The sheep huddle closely,

the last light leaves the sky.
I name this, Death.
His whisper stirs the flock,
lambs mew plaintively,
a nightbird carries the cry.
He hears it echo infinitely,
Hebron Valley, Cave Hill.

Begotten

All that talk of *ANCESTRY**
and I'm shy: bonsai pedigree,
branchy enough close to home,
comes up short at the head –
stones of Annabella Emerson,
my Scots-Presbyterian granny,
and Kitty Sandys Carroll,
my Father's Ma. Her teeth lived
under her pillow, with a naggin of
Paddy, and a handful of florins
she swore the tooth fairy brought.

Both lie with feet to the Mournes
in a churchyard in Louth; that's as far
as this ancestry thing has got me.
There was talk how Great-Uncle Joe
went to sea, on the *POWHATAN*
sailed for Virginia. *Promise you'll mind
the poor dog*, begged his last
to Grandad Frank, and *wait till
I've saved for a business*, remained
theirs sincerely, *Joe*, never to be
heard from again. So that's it then,

forced back on reserves: family
secrets Aunt Catherine fed me
as she hundred-stroked my hair:
Cearbhaill, the last King of Tara,
and our ancestor Hugh O'Neill.
We've a look of Cardinal Conway,
not to mention the Tribes of Israel.
Brought to the pin of my collar,
I fall back on Bryan MacMahon:
*There are only twenty-five old men
between each one of us and Christ.*

**ANCESTRY*, poems by Rajandaye Ramkissoon-Chen

1993

Conor O'Callaghan was born in Newry, Co. Down,
in 1968. His first collection of poems, *The History of Rain*
(The Gallery Press 1993), which won the Patrick Kavanagh
Poetry Award, was also short-listed for the Forward Best
First Collection Prize in 1994. A second collection, *Seatown*,
was published by Gallery in April 1999 and by Wake Forest
University Press, USA, in 2000.

He was writer-in-residence with University College Dublin
for 1999/2000, with Dun Laoghaire/Rathdown County
Council for 2000/1, and was director of the annual Poetry
Now Festival in Dun Laoghaire for 2001–3. During the 2004
spring semester he co-held with his wife, poet Vona
Groarke, the Heimbold Chair in Irish Studies at Villanova
University, Philadelphia.

A non-fiction book about the controversy surrounding
Ireland's involvement in the 2002 World Cup, entitled
Red Mist, was published by Bloomsbury in 2004. A third
collection of poems, *Fiction*, will appear in spring 2005.

The Ocean

We wanted to go to the ocean
to undress and make love,
so drove across the hottest afternoon
on record with the sun roof

wide open to where you were sure
would be a deserted cove.
But found miles from anywhere
that it wasn't entirely unheard of.

We agreed to take the plunge
as far from the crowd as possible.
We dared each other to change
without once using a towel.

At one point we just lay
at the edge of the surf in togs
and tried to get carried away.
It was useless. Too many dogs,

and fathers in snorkel and flippers,
and kids playing football
and scorched day trippers
watching from *The Blue Yonder Hotel.*

In the end we drove home
the same evening, and arrived late
to find the kitchen and living-room
had absorbed the city's heat.

I'd say we both remember this
when something in the small hours gives,
or when a train behind the house
passes like a handful of waves.

Green Baize Couplets

1

A handshake, a lowered light, the chance to clear her table
with what at first glance would appear to be a natural double.

2

Her colours on their spots, the cue-ball positioned perfectly ...
Under normal circumstances, this would be a formality.

3

Still she rattles on. What I would give for a referee's voice
to bellow from the shadows an authoritative 'Quiet, please'.

4

A consummate technician, with one eye on the score,
intent on not over-reaching, keeping one foot on the floor.

5

Fallen beyond arm's length, I begin to feel the tension,
throw my eyes to heaven, and ask for the extension.

6

A sip of something on ice, having left it in the jaws,
to the horror of yours truly, the absence of applause.

7

After her kiss on the green, my unexpected cannon,
we go to the mid-session interval with honours pretty much even.

8

A hint of gentle side, a couple of messed-up plants,
a kick, a longish pink, and the glimpse of a second chance.

9

However long it takes, we'll continue this black ball fight
though by now the heat is off and the meter has run out.

10

Just as you join us, she has given me a shot to nothing,
and I am about to reply by pinning her to the cushion.

Gloves

Making out with you
with the lights up full
might as well feel
like thinking
about the dark
inside of gloves.
I love that,
the lining unravelled,
your fingers' smell.
I even learn to love
the fluorescent strip
stammering to life,
the fact that fucking
might as well be
the only way we have
of looking down the barrel
at the gaps in the cold.
Then you take off,
and snow might as well fall
for years on end,
and yours are still
knotted or rolled
on the dumbwaiter
on the landing –
even after all
the bulbs have blown
and you've tried on
that excuse to return
once too often
and the room
has changed hands –
the left pushing the right
inside out.

The Oral Tradition

You've heard it
   a million times before –
the one about
   ships in the night
where two perfect
   strangers find
that a few words
   and the air of a song
handed down from when
   the world was young
aren't all they share.
   So much so
it becomes increasingly
   hard to swallow.
It seems only proper
   to make off
in the opposite
   direction rather
than go along
   with the certainty
that one thing
   will naturally
lead to another.
   Then, after an age
hiking over miles
   of featureless land
in a dead heat,
   a receptionist
in a coastal town
   offers rolls and beer
after hours,
   bores you to tears
with stories of her
   mother and uncles
in the mountains,
   and you think
that perhaps you
   should just toe

the line after all.
   She seems unsure
but undresses in your
   bathroom anyway
and cries for home
   when you kiss
a gradual ache
   between her legs.
Two men in the hall
   speaking double-dutch
and a squad car
   throwing violets on
the wall at dawn
   are all you'll recount
of the point when
   you in turn
come in her mouth.
   The following day
is the longest
   for many years.
She pays both fares
   on the bus inland
to where the trees
   and sun suddenly
are much higher
   and much warmer
than you can even
   begin to say.

The Count

There's this pal of a pal who earned his stripes
snipping surplus nipples from made-for-TV flicks.
As little as six or seven frames a piece,
they curled in a box at his feet like locks of hair
or like shavings planed from a strip of maple.

Me? I like to think I get my kicks elsewhere.
Still, his nickname lingers on the tip of my tongue
whenever I lose all hope of something worth seeing
and hit the standby through a late double bill,
or whenever I cut my teeth on a sweet red apple.

1994

Celia de Fréine is a poet, dramatist and screenwriter
who writes in Irish and English. She was born in
Newtownards, Co. Down, and now lives in Dublin and in
Connemara.

Many of her plays have been staged, including most
recently, *Nára Turas é in Aistear*. *Anraith Neantóige* won
the Oireachtas na Gaeilge award for best play in 2003. For
several years she scripted the TG4 soap opera *Ros na Rún*.

Since 1994 Celia de Fréine has been concentrating mainly
on writing poetry in Irish and has won many awards,
including the Duais Chomórtas Filíochta Dhún Laoghaire
(1996), the British Comparative Literature Association
Translation Award (1999), Duais Aitheantais Ghradam
Litríochta Chló Iar-Chonnachta (1999) and the Smurfit
International Award for best Irish poem, Samhain Poetry
Festival, Gort a' Choirce (2003).

A collection *Faoi Chabáistí is Ríonacha* (Cló Iar-Chonnachta
2001) has been translated into Bulgarian and Romanian and
a new sequence of poems *Fiacha Fola* is due in 2004. She is
currently working on a volume of poetry in English, entitled
Scarecrows at Newtownards. 'In the Land of Wince and
Whinny' from this collection came second in the New Writer
Competition.

Cherubin, My Eye

He's up to his old tricks again –
drawing down forks of lightning,
making the ocean heave and groan

like a birthing sow, only this time
it's worse – he keeps muttering how
some bastard duke cast him and me –

a cherubin – adrift in a barque
of seeping wood. It's late – I can do
without being dragged out of bed

to witness another drowning hulk.
There was a time when we used
to dash in and out of the ocean,

daring the waves to swallow us up.
Then the weather changed and he took
to building this ramshackle hut.

Once ensconced with his telescope
and books, my education began –
geometry, chemistry, Greek,

the study of lunar phases,
but I can't fathom how, on the eve
of each new moon, there's blood

and pain, and I think I'm going to die.
Look at him standing there in the rain,
his bald patch purple and wet.

Next thing he'll catch cold
and we'll have the amphibian creep
in at all hours, ferrying logs.

Ere yesterday when rummaging
among the rubble that is my room
I came across a picture of a creature

I think might be a man. I hid him
and during the night sneaked him out
and ran my fingers through his hair.

Heavy Weather

When the wind is at its highest I can
feel her tug at the quilt, her fingers light
on the felt appliquéd rose at the base
of my spine. As it abates I hear her
whimper behind the wainscot and can't but
remember how a friend once visited
a medium, who summoned his mother
and bade her say what he needed to hear.

Not for me this conversation between
worlds. I'd sooner leave the door ajar, watch
the landing light shaft motes into the room,
listen to the stairs gasp beneath each step,
as others that were here before, wander
up and down in search of sanctuary.

Let Him Skip Hence

What if I was enamoured of an ass –
Oberon had become a bore of late
and when he started on those same crass
jokes and tiresome stories I couldn't wait

to head for my neck of the wood, little
thinking he'd trail behind like a lovesick
schoolboy, smear me with oxalic spittle
aided and abetted by that sidekick

of his. I'll have any sprite I fancy
wherever and whenever I like. Rue
the day I met the wretch. He'll not bring me
to heel. I could tell you a thing or two

about that night of unbridled passion –
only such deeds have gone out of fashion.

In the Land of Wince and Whinny
(At St James's Hospital)

I hear souls shriek, whips crack, and by degrees,
make out the shunting of a copier
on speed. The computed-tomography-
scan snaps poems I have written, poems

I have yet to write. Those of you who don't
believe in an afterlife, this is how
it feels. And when all my subjects have been
predicated, all my images spliced,

the mouth of the void spews me out. Cackles
whirligig after me to the café
where I take refuge in a vanilla

slice. Beside me a stroke-survivor smiles.
I caress her blue-fleeced shoulder and kiss
her blue-blonde head faster than the speed of life.

Just Dessert in Gran Canaria

Why feel affronted when called the English
woman? I did consult the Union Jack
section of the menu. The short waiter
saw me – it was he handed me the menu
open at that very page. The sparkles
on the ice cream almost singed my sweatshirt

as he ran past. It's my mother's sweatshirt,
as it happens. Now, she was an English
woman, from Londonderry, a bright spark
whose father fought under the Union Jack.
I peruse other flags on the menu
but in the end order from the waiter

sirloin steak, chips, and salad. The waiter
jots down my order, brushes my sweatshirt
as he leans over, collects the menu.
No! I couldn't possibly look English,
could I? I glower at my husband, Jack.
He shrugs and laughs and points at the sparkling

desserts. 'Bring my wife one of those sparkling
ice creams, a big one,' he tells the waiter.
He's always trying to please me, dear Jack.
He wouldn't notice which wretched sweatshirt
I was wearing – whether it was English
or not. He's not annoyed by the menu

and doesn't understand why the menu
should make my blood boil and my eyes sparkle.
No, seriously, do I look English –
I want to shout across at the waiter.
Perhaps he saw me slip off the sweatshirt
and noticed it boasted a Union Jack

label, and then flicked to the Union Jack
page, he being used to opening menus
and seeing labels on backs of sweatshirts
as he runs between tables with sparkling
desserts. Could those other busy waiters
tell the difference between an English

woman and a Jackeen? I like sparkling
desserts, choice menus, but can't abide waiters
who almost singe sweatshirts and call me English.

1995

William Wall is a poet and fiction writer who lives in
Cork. Born in 1955, he was educated at University College
Cork. His three novels, *Alice Falling*, *Minding Children* and
The Map of Tenderness, were published by Hodder/Sceptre,
London. His short fiction has appeared in places as diverse
as *Phoenix Irish Short Stories*, RTÉ and *Carve Magazine*.

His first poetry collection, *Mathematics and Other Poems*
(The Collins Press 1997) contained all the poems that won
the Patrick Kavanagh Poetry Award. A second volume of
poetry, *Fahrenheit Says Nothing To Me*, was published by
The Dedalus Press in 2004. William Wall has won many
literary prizes, including three Listowel Writers'
Week/American Ireland Fund Awards for poetry and short
fiction and the inaugural Sean O'Faolain Award.

'*From* the Wake in the House' and 'Radiance' are from
Mathematics and Other Poems; the other three poems are
from his second collection. 'The Wasps' Nest' won the
Listowel prize for best individual poem in 1997.

from The Wake in the House

Lastly comes a clearing. The rain has gone.
& it was not the soft spring rain. It was
a slant & winter rain. The hardest thing?
That the house was not empty when we
came home. Emptiness was what we expected.
We expected the hollow sounding rain
on the kitchen windows. Instead there were
wardrobes of her clothes to be disposed,
the set of her shoulders in them, hairs on
collars, crocodile leather handbags, fur boots.
We put order on them, talking in stiff
whispers. Breath-catching loneliness.
Then we laid them out for the last time,
A family of black plastic bags on the road.

Radiance

The jets fly over our house at night,
three lights, heeled slightly to the east,
& the noise of movement follows them
        briefly into the stars.

Sometimes we hold hands on the garden-seat
like Victorian lovers waiting for an eclipse
for privacy, psychologists of air, trembling
        at every windchange.

We imagine the passengers, faces bleached
against the glass, descending into deafness.
They are looking down at the radiant berries
        of our cotoneasters.
        We are their stars.

The Stairs Unlit

I stumble from a dream
in too many rooms
& stop
finding the stairs unlit.

These years later
I must find
the necessary light
descending into darkness

where I found her
as she had been for hours
staring at the rain.
When all the ways are dark

we see at the edge
the edge of things
the city shrouded
in dust & smoke

& the dead come
young men & girls
the bride & bridegroom
our ghosts.

Alfred Russell Wallace in the Molluccas

Alfred Russell Wallace in the Molluccas
I know his pain. Night after night
in the light of his specimens
ague & mortification
& the sheer variety of things.
The world is staggering
a sickness itself an infested planet
heedless of reason meaningless hotchpotch.

Then one night the brutal fact
borne in upon him (the fittest survive).
In the meantime there are ulcers
& malaria perhaps gangrene
& all of this to be skinned & shipped
& a letter to Darwin to give the game away.

The Wasps' Nest

Ho paura someone said
& I fear greatly
on a dark night
when the wind is a fiddle-bridge
sounding the body

(your cheek resting on that certain curve
with nonchalance).

My father was a self-taught man
he held the fiddle loosely like a girl in a reel
uncertain of the next note

& he was afraid as the strokes
ate out his brain.

Remember the wasp-nest
that grew under the rafters
the beauty of the hanging shape
a chinese lantern.
He bore it before him on a hayfork
humming
but it cast no light.

I was charged with opening doors
looking inside & out.
I saw the way he held his head high
tilted like a robin's

but I could not foresee
the fuses going one by one
until the house was dark.

It's true what they say
winter & the small hours
take the older ones
there is always some funeral or other
yes

& the death of fathers is common.
Look out for the early crocus
he used to say
new lambs like paper bags scattered in the grass
soul-rags on a barbed-wire fence
for death cometh soon or late
the keeper of secrets
scrambling among trinkets
immortal stories.

He could throw nothing out
but the salvage of small things
did not protect him.

Lovers are specialists
trawling for hope
as my father did
as my mother did.

Remember how they would swing away
waltzing on eggshells
his hand on her waist
the happy dancers
conducting their own silence
through the crowded night
the thunderous sky?

(What I am afraid of
is that it is not empty.)

The wind goes down to a bass-viol
in an empty warehouse.
Where are the stars?

We learn that birds sing
long before dawn
& rain in the doorway is soft.

An old wrinkled potato is the soul
growing up with death
& there is toxin there

(they got their teeth in us alright).
So considering the evidence
there is no escape

unless it be you & me
stretched out like spoons in a drawer
sheltering each other.

1996

Bill Tinley was born in Chicago in 1965. His family

moved to Ireland in 1970 and he was educated at Maynooth
University, where he currently works as conference manager.
He recently completed his doctoral thesis on the poetry of
Derek Mahon. He is married and has three sons.

He began publishing poetry while at university and a selec-
tion of his work appeared in *Raven Introductions 4* (1986).
In 1990 he published *Opera Minima*, a trilingual booklet of
poems, with the Milanese poet, Edoardo Zuccato. *Chess in
the Afternoon*, translations from the Hungarian of Olga
Czilczer, was published in 1998 in collaboration with Thomas
Kabdebo. Bill Tinley's poems have appeared in Ireland (*The
Irish Times, Poetry Ireland Review, Metre, The SHOp*), the
UK (*Stand, Agenda*), the USA (*Poetry, TriQuarterly, The
Formalist, The Literary Review, Sparrow*), Canada (*The
Fiddlehead*), Belgium (*De Braake Hond*) and South Africa
(*Carapace*). His first collection, *Grace*, was published by
New Island Books in 2001. His poems have been translated
into Italian, Spanish and Hungarian and anthologized in
Stream and Gliding Sun (1998) and *The Backyards of
Heaven* (2003).

Danaë

after Klimt

You wake up in a glitter of gold dust,
On your skin the rainbow of love's dry stain,
A jangle in your head the ring of lust.
This morning you will not be calmed by rain
That nourishes the roses and the rust,

You won't find consolation in the cry
Of distant birds nor in the breeze's song
Hear more than what the clouded palm of sky
Predicts – indifferent to right and wrong
The gods who make destroy and do not die.

Epithalamium

for David and Sally

You won't recall, or wish to, later on
The morning heat, the skin's first tongue of sweat
Beneath the unworn dress, the spotless suit,
The ordinary nature of the sun
And all it shines on. If you rose early
When the streets were still and from your window
Watched as timorous pigeons necked below
You might have chosen this for memory.

And though the lovers tired of their love
Before you turned away, before you dressed,
Before the sun had scorched the sky above,
You will remember nothing of the rest
Since you must choose today to keep at bay
Whatever doubts undo a wedding day.

First Thoughts on the Death of Joseph Brodsky
on my paperback edition of *To Urania*

Foreshadowing time's handiwork on stone,
Creases and dog-ears spawn like spider lace
On the photograph of sister Muses,
Like wrinkles on the writer's weary face

Or the complicated biography
Embroidered in the palm of his closed hand.
The battered accumulation of lines
Amounts to zero substance in the end.

The book will crumble like that sisterhood,
Depositing its crumpled celloglaze,
Its scattered gatherings and orphaned leaves
As dust in the furrows of future days.

For the moment, though, it remains intact,
Its sagging torso and weathered physique
Signs of pocket travel, its signatures
Like ink moles dedicated to a cheek.

So what if destiny condemns it to
The fate of acid rained-on bronze and stone?
Time's appetite does not discriminate
Between the paper and the finger-bone.

None of this nostalgia will redeem us.
It's looking up from the line's excesses,
From the long street's lack of a horizon,
Knowing that tomorrow's crevices

Are filling up with dust as fate decrees,
It's looking up, gauging the perspective,
Not flinching from one's reflection that counts,
Seeking in the face of death a way to live.

Aubade, Winter

A freight train slows to fifteen through the town and choos.
Officially it's dawn, but in the darkness who's
To know? Birds won't sing in these forsaken milieus.

Instead, what wakes you is that engine's huff-and-puff
Or else, next door, your neighbour's smoke-and-coffee cough.
The radio alarm squats, waiting to go off.

It's the wrong side of seven and too late to snooze.
Not quite on the ball yet you miss the early news,
The weather forecast, the morning paper reviews.

Beside you, duvet wrapped up round her like a ruff,
Your wife half-stirs, rolls over in a dozy huff.
Distantly, in lieu of chirps, a mongrel's woof-woof.

Daybreak on the roller-blind is a week-old bruise
Gone yellow and ochre and a spectrum of blues,
Leaking just sufficient light on trousers and shoes

To bring it almost back – the striptease to your buff,
The candle's nervous flame, and when you'd had enough,
At sleep's behest, the day extinguished with a snuff.

And suddenly, as if they've overheard you muse,
Your eldest's up, the youngest shakes the cot and coos.
Come on. It's time to rise and shine. How could you refuse?

Gethsemane Revisited

Some day, when all of this is through,
When I have supped my medicine,
Been doubled-crossed by you-know-who
And three times been denied; have risen,
Gone to ground, returned and said adieu;

When finally I've been forgotten –
In a millennium or, let's say, two –
Remind me to come back again,
A godforsaken inconnu,
For one more hour in this garden;

Unrecognized at last by Jew
Or Gentile, in Ray-Bans, shaven,
With backpack guide in neo-Hebrew
Close at hand, a Fuji, 7-
Up and bar, I'll marvel at the view

Of Calvary, the Mount, the Jordan,
Old Jerusalem – and not a queue
In sight; a private citizen,
I'll shake a pebble from my shoe,
Kick back, doze off, top up my tan.

Yes, something to look forward to.
But first things first. Whatever's written
Must be done and falls to me to do.
High time I woke my merry men.
And here comes Judas, right on cue.

Tennis Courts in Snow

Snow has come down since dawn
On the first Saturday
Of Hilary mid-term

And now in the clear gaze
Of a night sky speckled
Full of moonlight and stars

The tennis courts are laid
Out smooth as a towel,
Whiter than Wimbledon,

The sagging nets forlorn
And all the lines erased
By inches of this fall.

Beneath it, scuff-marked outs
And dodgy service calls,
A rally's join-the-dots

Intact across the grit,
A backhand passing shot,
An ace at forty-love.

Beyond the frozen fence
A sodium spotlight
Spreads its Lucozade glow,

The solitary hint
Of sunrise or of sunset,
Of summertime to come.

1997

Michael McCarthy was born in 1945 and grew up
on the family farm in Rerahanagh, West Cork. He studied for
the priesthood at St Patrick's College, Carlow, and was
ordained in 1969. Since then he has lived mainly in England.
During a year spent studying spirituality in Chicago in
1987–8 he discovered his poetic self. While teaching at St
Cuthbert's Seminary, Durham, from 1988–96, he began
writing poetry.

His first poem was published in 1995 when he was fifty. Two
years later he won the Patrick Kavanagh Poetry Award.
Birds' Nests and Other Poems, based on the award-winning
collection, was published by Bradshaw Books in 2003. He
has also published two books of verse for children with
Barefoot Books, *The Story of Noah and the Ark* and *The
Story of Daniel in the Lions' Den*. The first of these has been
translated into seventeen languages.

Michael McCarthy now lives in North Yorkshire where he
works as a parish priest. He is currently preparing a second
poetry collection.

Birds' Nests

We learned about God
from birds' nests; from those
tabernacles perched in a hedge,
hidden between moss-covered stones
in a ditch, or under the lip of some ledge.

When you found one, it was a secret
you kept to yourself. I had seven that were mine.
My brother had more but he was bigger than me
and anyway crows didn't count. They were too high up.
You had to be able to see into them. My uncle lifted me up
to see into one that had blue eggs in it. That counted alright.
My mother said the one I showed her was a robin's nest.
Her breast was red because she had felt sorry for Our Lord
on the cross and blood dripped from the nail onto her breast
and the spot never came off.

You had to whisper. It was like being in Church.
Touching the eggs was a sin.
It was like lifting a girl's skirt.
I put my hand in once
just to see how they felt. They were
smooth like my sister's hair
warm like her skin.
I told it in confession, said I'd never do it again.

Donegan lived near the school.
He said birds' nests were a cod.
He robbed the one in the wall,
stuck his hand right into the hole
it came out with the eggs in his fist.
We could hear the cracking of shells
see the ooze through his fingers like sick.
His face had a crooked look.

He wiped the egg off his hand on Mary Driscoll's dress.

Sam Gosling's Corner

Sam Gosling's orchard was hidden
in the growth behind the grain loft.
The trick would be to wake Sam first,
not have him woken by a squall of cats.
Our bare feet made no sound
on the cold flagged floor,

there was only the ticking of the clock
and Sam's afternoon snore.
'What's the time Sir?'
(The Master said his name was Mister Gosnell
and we should call him Sir.)
'What's the time Sir?' 'Half past three,' he said.

The apple trees were friendly,
familiar like his trousers of grey frieze.
We took an apple each and ran
back past his house, and heard him
talking to himself: 'Isn't that the devil now
the kettle boiled, the tay ready, and no bread.'

We ate them all the way to Kingston's bridge,
compared our teeth marks on the cores;
then raced them down the river at the count of three.
Mine was winning till it sank.
You could tell an apple from its taste
we said. Sam's tasted, sort of, Protestant.

Shop apples seduced us after that.
They were from foreign parts,
had painted lips and polished skin.
Their taste had no religion.

The Gift

And love, she said, was not
waiting for what had been expected
but more like listening to the river
that ran beneath your skin

was not the silver birch
spine stiff with anticipation
but more like the shiver of its leaves
upturned in the mid-morning wind.

And love, she said, was not
the breaking of some stone ghost
but more like the sound of water ebbing.
It came, she said, like a slow tide.

It crept across the shadows of trees
through the open skylight
into the bedroom of the boy
while his memory lay sleeping.

It came, she said
touching the space between his eyebrows,
fixing in his dark dreams
the broken axle to the wheel.

In Memoriam

Let's say the year is Twenty-One-Sixteen.
The headstone says I died in Twenty-Thirty-Six.
Though I've been dead these eighty years
I'm pleased to see I lived to ninety-one.

The graveyard perched
above an S of sea where boats can rest
along a lonely curve of shore
where tourists no longer come.

Beneath my name, the dates of birth and death
some long-forgotten lines I haven't written yet.
Beside my grave a grass-grown gravel path
unused except by fishermen at night.

I see a woman, pushing back the grass.
She's twenty-five or so.
Researching for her PhD, her subject:
Forgotten Irish Poets.
She found some poems of mine on micro-disk
buried in the archives of a library
in Edmonton Alberta, where
I was almost famous once.

She stands among small raindrops
as I once stood
in the graveyard at Drumcliff.
She weeps as I wept over Yeats.

A strand of hair clings to her face.
A briar sways in unnoticed wind.
Far below the waves say hush.
Close by a blackbird sings.

After the Wedding

I leave the revellers at midnight.
Southbound on the M6 the phone rings
and before answering it, I know.

At 9.30 pm tonight my mother died.

The car cruises, the curve of the wipers
responding to sporadic showers.
My engines have shut down.

Dull at the edges, raw in the centre
I can feel my toes tingle.
Yesterday she sat out in the sun.

I wait an hour, then call you.
I hear the texture of your voice
as you retell each moment slowly.

This morning she said to you 'I'm dying'
and you asked 'are you afraid?'
She told you she was not.

After the priest had come and blessed her
with the final rites, the day went quietly.
She slept a little now and then.

In the evening she told Ita she was going.
'Maybe I'll wait until the morning.'
In the event she didn't.

At 95 years, and conscious to the last
her breathing stopped. I ask about
distress. You say there was none.

Arriving home at 3.00 am, there are
nine messages on my Ansaphone.
I don't need to answer them.

I check the internet for flights, then walk outside.
In awhile I hear the first birds sing.
Memories begin.

1998

Carmel Fitzsimons was born in 1959, the eldest of a family of eleven children. Due to the paucity of job opportunities in rural Ireland in the fifties and sixties her parents, Patrick Fitzsimons from Westmeath and Moira O'Reilly from Cavan, emigrated to London. The family was almost absurdly upwardly mobile and all the children went on to take degrees.

Carmel studied English Literature at Somerville College, Oxford, before joining the *Cambridge Evening News* as a journalist. She returned to London to work as a reporter and feature writer with the *Observer*. She now has four children and freelances for the *Guardian*. She also works closely with local primary schools, holding weekly poetry workshops to increase children's awareness of their own poetic abilities.

When she won the Patrick Kavanagh Poetry Award she wanted to do something magical with the winnings. She bought a horse called Hercules who loves to gallop across the fields of Meath and Westmeath. 'Who says poetry can't take you anywhere?'

Bombers

Baghdad was a book I had at school,
With pictures obscured by thin transparent papers
That crumpled as they turned. Turquoise as strange
As the word itself, vivid pinks so thick you could peel them
Off the page. Funny fat men in turbans with big bellies
Flopping over balloon trousers, which were caught at the ankle
And finished off with long curling shoes like the tendrils
Of creeping honeysuckle. Women with strange noses and wisps
Of veils, floating with their arms folded, on flying carpets
Over turreted buildings sculpted out of ice-cream.
The night the war began I went to bed alone and woke
To my husband's gentle touch. 'Do not be afraid,' he said
'But they are bombing Baghdad.' The winter light filtered
In through the blinds with a lunar glow and I felt as small
As a child in her parents' bedroom, waking to find the adults
Have left her alone in a room she no longer knew.

Bonnard

He washed her hair. That, more than all the other services
Of groin and limbs is the one, in its connubial intimacy, that
Troubled her most. The soapy massage as she lay like a Bonnard's
Bather, alight in the simmering lucidity of a just-loved body.
Her mother had said she must take more care of herself
Sleeping night after night on a camp bed. So he anointed her,
Saying forget clinical corridors and rubber soled angels of fear.
Now it's the lapping of the sudsy wave and those strong fingers
Seeking the place where the hairline and its fractures start.
And there are the meals barely eaten. Pudding? No. Coffee? No.
Another drink. There is a richer wine at my place.
Back to hours of passion and sitting naked, quoting Larkin.
Getting out diaries to fill the velvet month of dalliance.
Empty poems and promises he carries. Think of her with the
    closet of grief
She hauls around every day like Sisyphus up the hill.
Think how she lay, entombed in his bath, just before he slipped
In like a misshapen bar of soap behind her. Did his lips dry
With the words of untrue love he had spoken to her?
What bath, what stream, what sea, what ocean
Would ever clean such a stain as this from him?

Clothes

I went back to Oxford Street for the little black suit
With the Edwardian waist and the skirt that's so
Like a ripple breathing on to a silent Scottish shore.
If January had not misered me I would have insinuated
Myself into it on the bright morning of our candle-lit lunch.
It still clasps me like squeezing hands up on a ribcage trapeze,
And it still trickles across the thighs like sweat at midnight.
But the girl in the glass smiles back in a different month.
Lips plump from kissing, eyes drowning with the promise
Of a marriage of moans in a private treaty of darkness.
It was she who made me buy the black lace sheath of a dress
With the primrose dalliance lining. The one which the shop
Girls stillettoed around, cooing like pigeons, saying it looks
As if you've absolutely nothing underneath. And
So versatile for nibbling a cocktail cherry with the dry-lipped
Ambassador or for counting the honey bubbles lazing up
A lager glass on a summer afternoon in a pub by a river.
And then, while they scattered their compliments like bread-
    crumbs
In Trafalgar Square, I raided the bank. I bought;
The sticky black leggy dress the porn tailor had razored up the
    side.
The cobweb chemise that flutters like a moth. The delicate two
    piece
That is a duet of summer swimming pools. Powder, baby,
Sky-blue blue for a July afternoon of wet fingers
Trailing the wake of the waters that drift past
The colleges. A brazen pair of sunglasses nudged themselves
Into the company of the bags tumbling with black satin,
And buttery silk and the washed innocence of newborn
Cornflowers lost in a field of hypnotic poppies.
'These', I said, to my teasing and excitable new cupboard loves.
'These, my darlings, are the clothes of a newly-wed.'
Or the costumes of an actress.

Love Lets You Go; For My Father

We will see you walking in the early evening
Along the little hills and roads of Tonyshammer.
In the Spring when the lanes whiten
And the trees make a network across the skies.
In the Summer's slanting sunlight amidst the dipping swallows
Where the roses swoon in the slow afternoons.
In the Autumn, with extra cardigans against the chill.
Always rabbiting, whooping the terriers across the fields.
We will glimpse you in the Winter, moonlight on your brow
Checking the starshine and the outside light.
We see you waiting by the wall, balanced like a dancer
With your cap tilted and old stick in hand,
Waiting for the stragglers and the strays,
Ready to discuss the wind and weather
Or the inner workings of a bicycle wheel.
We will touch your lovely pianist's fingers
And try to make the perfect cup of tea.
We will debate the management of the range
And the perfidy and trickery of politicians.
You will be the spirit of the places you built and loved
You will roll up your trousers and paddle in the sea.
You will carefully polish the glasses at another party
And waltz once more across the shining floor
With the true love of your life within your arms.
Love lets you go but holds you close forever.
And in a golden evening we will walk together
Along the little hills and roads of home.

A Lullaby for Ellie

In the cool of the summer evening they are counting the cows
On the Ben of Fore. Far up the hills the white boulders turn
Slow heads, becoming muscle before turning back to stone.
The late sun slants along the meadows that wash round
The boggy skirts of the ruined abbey. Rabbits' tails
Skitter like a flash of white robes late for Matins, as they burrow
Down the earthy dark cathedrals branching beneath the grass.
Your footsteps crunch the lane, your laughter echoing out to the
    horses.
You are raising fences, lugging planks, tipping tyres for a
    makeshift arena.
A girl show-jumper with red hair that forever conspires its
    startling escape.
On the dresser last year's gold rosettes from the Oldcastle Show
Dangle against the milk dipped blue cups, against the statue of
    Our Lady
Mysterious in her dome of faded crystal. Here you pressed flowers,
Drank cocoa, played cards at a tilting table until your sleepy body
Had to be levered into the blackness of the star threshed night.
Above on Slieve na Caillaigh the megalithic stones store up
    centuries
Across their cold granite folds. The uncut grasses whisper around
    them
Of the brave mother carrying the baby up the unrelenting hills,
While you pressed eagerly on, revelling in the eiderdown
Of fields and hedges, a toy country spread beneath your serious
    gaze.
You walked the Yew Tree walk where Blessed Oliver trod out
Across the crippled junctions of the roots of tree and history,
His office and his preparations for his early death.
Those trees, age-old companions of graveyard grief, bent down
To shade you as you stepped into what we thought would be
A future of clear rounds and trophies from the Aga Khan.
Instead our summer has withered into winter
As Persephone leaves before her time. The places that she loved,
And that have loved her, have cast off sun and summer glow
And let rain and wind and bitter chill batter June into a winter
    grief.

The Ben of Fore, Ballinacree, the lakes of Lene and Sheelin,
    Slieve na Caillaigh,
All night have been rain and water churning in their hearts' core.
But, in the evening light, through the long shadows she walks
    there still.
She walks across rough hills, hands full of apples, red hair plaited
Like new French bread. But she does not walk alone.
Now it is her father who holds her hand and they, investigators
    to the wind and spray,
At last begin to fathom the never fathomed Seven Wonders of Fore.

I wish ...

I wish I was your toothbrush, or the crumple in a linen suit
Which hopeful fingers probe for buried treasure. I wish
I was your anniversary model, gripped like a steering wheel,
Spinning down wet splashy roads of reflecting winter rain,
I wish I were the glass doors of an unresisting tall office
As you push through to start your working day. I wish I wore
A naval pullover with self-important major-domo epaulettes.
I'd frown at all the morning people coming in but when you arrived
I'd smile and say, 'There is no need for your pass, dear.
You can access all departments and ride up in any lift.'
I wish I was the coat you throw across your chair. The coffee cup
Your hands encircle and the cigarette your lighter's lighting.
I wish I was your computer keyboard, submissive on your desk
Waiting for the touch of a piano man's fingers to tap across
The rise and fall of me. I wish I was Evelyn and Claire and Aoife,
Sinead, and all the ones you tease and boss and telephone.
I wish I was your date for the dinner dance tonight.
I would be twenty-eight with a schoolgirl smile and Mata Hari
    style,
With my hair worn up and my décolletage worn down, in a dress
That would lick my legs like a cat's tongue and flutter across
Unchiselled shoes with Forties' straps indenting silk stockings.
The tablecloth would lie like a bed sheet between us
And our party would wonder who this shiny couple could be.
Companions in star-gazing madness eventually liquefying
Into a midnight taxi away from the envying crowd. And maybe
    then
I think I'd know you'd know how much I wish I was your tooth-
    brush.

1999

Eibhlín Nic Eochaidh

Born and brought up in Bray, Co. Wicklow, Eibhlín Nic Eochaidh moved to Glenfarne, Co. Leitrim, in 1979 and stayed. She lives there with her husband, Gearóid. She recently graduated from the MPhil course in Creative Writing at Trinity College. Since her return from Dublin she has worked as an arts advisor in creative writing on a pilot partnership project between the Arts Office and the Yeats Society, Sligo. She is a member of the Knocknarea Writers, Sligo.

Eibhlín Nic Eochaidh's poetry has been published in *Contrasts* (ed. Brian Leyden, 1996), *Women's Work*, *IX* (1998), *Dogs Shot from Cannons* (Wholly Trinity Press 2000), *Staying Alive*, *Real Poems for Unreal Times* (ed. Neil Astley, 2002), *Badal* (ed. Noel Monahan, 2003), and in *Force 10*, *College Green*, *Poetry Ireland Review*, *Cyphers* and *Cúirt* 2003 and 2004. She participated in the first Rattlebag Poetry Slam during the Dublin Literary Festival, 2001, and is one of the featured writers in *The Living Word* (Town House 2001).

The first two poems anthologized here are from the un-published collection that won the Patrick Kavanagh Poetry Award.

On Learning to Read

Her eldest son
learned to read
from a Dr Seuss book –
Are-You-My-Mother?

Did you ever look
into the faces of women
and think –
Are you my mother?

Did you wonder
how I looked?
Was my hair long?
Why did I abandon you?

I reach out
and touch your face
and hear your voice
echo in my head.

You speak so low
I barely catch a thread –
even your silence
sings.

Her Blue Cardigan

Today I burned my mother's old blue cardigan.
My mother is ten years dead.
She wore the blue cardigan
at night in bed, while she read.
I am the only daughter whose ears are pierced.
After her death I kept her gold earrings,
her hand-sewing machine, the copper jug
she put flowers in
and her old blue cardigan.

Reading in bed in winter,
wind whistling through the gable window,
it kept me warm. The cat curled up on it,
slipping in behind my back
on early mornings. Today
I burned my mother's old blue cardigan.
It smelled like human hair.

What She Remembers Now

is her ironic recognition
of the plant edging the path
in the garden – helxine, baby's tears;

the way two Irish accents made her head turn,
the narrow stairway to the upper room
and a familiar waiting, shuffling round the walls;

how she registered *after* by absence
of the travel poster on the ceiling:
last thing her eyes had seen *before*.

How to Kill a Living Thing

Neglect it
Criticize it to its face
Say how it kills the light
Traps all the rubbish
Bores you with its green

Continually
Harden your heart
Then
Cut it down close
To the root as possible

Forget it
For a week or a month
Return with an axe
Split it with one blow
Insert a stone

To keep the wound wide open.

Holding the Space

January. I stand and watch
two men walk over and back
behind lawnmowers, orange and green.

They are cutting grass
in the middle of playing fields,
making a rectangle, green on green.

I don't know why they're doing this.
For tennis courts in spring? –
Or why I've stopped to watch.

Something about the marked-out space,
the movements the men make.
This is their work.

Behind them, fencing protects a site:
Toyota van; brown plastic pipes;
grey portacabins with a yellow stripe.

All I see are men
methodically cutting blades of grass
marking out a kind of cleared space.

2000

Joseph Woods was born in Drogheda in 1966. He
studied biology and chemistry and worked for a few years as
a chemist. In 1991 he went to Asia and taught English in
Japan for two years; a further year was spent travelling
through Asia and Russia. He holds an MA in Creative
Writing from Lancaster University.

His poetry was first published in Japan and has since been
published and translated in journals and anthologies interna-
tionally. He has lectured and read in the UK, Italy, Sicily,
Austria, Russia and India. *Sailing to Hokkaido*, based on the
collection that won the Patrick Kavanagh Poetry Award, was
published by Worple Press, UK, in 2001. He is currently
working on a second collection to be published in spring
2005. Joseph Woods is the director of Poetry Ireland.

An Occasional House of Her Father's

You loped ahead over fields hardened
by winter, leading me to another secret
place; a cottage consented by your father.
When asked, he simply gave you the keys.

Until now, it had been strange gardens,
private meadows or your favourite table
tombs. And if they weren't secret
they became so, in the hours we visited.

Indoors, you showed me a painting
of a steamship belonging to some ancestor
who had grown up in a dream
of the sea, was swallowed by it.

I could smell apples as my fingers twilled
your hair. You opened your father's room,
bare except for apples. An entire floor
cobbled with windfalls, green as the door
we came through.

The care he had taken with each apple
to mould a practical tapestry for winter.
With a strand of that same care he would
return, winter done, to string himself
to silence and kick away the chair.

Landship

We're a gang or crew of four manning
this landship, gliding over and trawling
each drill. Inside, the broad-belt rungs
potatoes past to the drop of a hold.

Our hands don't touch the healthy:
only debris, the frostbitten ones
and last year's progenitors, the globes
of mucus that held until now.

Since lunch, enough pinks to feed a life.
Now our measure is full holds and trailers,
drawing toward farmyard lights. We work
on under a fluorescent lamp, divining.

Standing two aside in our canvas cabin,
lulled as time grows, we are quick
and our eyes have sharpened. Still drawn
by horsepower, nothing stops us

except nature; the hoarfrost or waterlogged ground.
I jump off for a piss as we veer near a hedgerow.
Crows have fled the black bronchiole
and vacated the clots of their own making.

I watch it pass, an ugly sailing junk
lit like a lantern. Voices from inside
warm the din as the tractor tows
the harvester down a dark slope,

to fresh drills. I have found my pitch
in this season of evictions.
A place on a moving belt above earth
with a part scraping it.

Interview

It dances on draughts
that do not disturb me,

a fleck of dust, soaring
the micro-Boreas of a corridor.

I was made wait, and the mind
idles over distance. Somewhere,

a Chaos-butterfly is flapping
its wings. I have no ear

for diminutive beats, and this tremble
is perceptible to the eye only.

Or perhaps a corridor is the bell jar
in that theory. I've attached myself

to dust and feel it in my bones –
if this fleck sinks from sight

it was a bird of ill omen.

A Carvery Lunch in Louth

Millions long for immortality who do not know
what to do with themselves on a rainy Sunday afternoon
Susan Ertz, *Anger In The Sky*, 1943

Here in the half-lit church of the Sunday carvery the nose smarts
with the sweat of an entire gymnasium of vegetables boiled
   beyond
belief. Colours washed into one sodden mass and the unshaven
   bacon
bristles the ring of fat that holds the bloodied beef together.
   Flashbacks
to cabbage and force-feeding. We queue for this, while others are
   lamped
by the wide-screen TV, staring through the thick air of *John
Player Blue*.
Today it might be the banner county, the wee county or the cats
   and a voice
commentates as if from under a wet newspaper. Childhood
   Sundays haunted
by that drone, coming from car-radios by the sea, where solitary
   men sat
in satori and summer heat. We take our poison, toddlers scream,
and grown-ups in acrylic green jerseys drink lager like milk,
in a culture of the coronary, some dispossession taking place.

Plastic Butterflies

To hold out in a room near the harbour
longing for you over eight time-zones
among your lagan as you'd left it
scattered around. Preferring the sound

of your clock to mine and putting
my own to your time. Your plastic
iridescent-butterfly-hairclip let lie
on the locker and a bracelet graced

the bookshelf. I went back to old ways,
leaving the radio on all night and stravaging
the pier at dusk between sea and sadness
adding to the cargo of ships departing,

attaching dreams to their prows and wondering
how letters ever reach their destinations.
To lie at night with curtains undrawn
be absolved by moonlight, and if a cloud

came to veil its halogen my heart would race
until it cleared again. That was a year of counting,
seeing signs in every subliminal,
while the garden crawled with magpies.

2001

Ann Leahy was born in Borrisoleigh, Co. Tipperary. At age seventeen she came to Dublin to attend university and still lives there. For many years she worked as a solicitor in private practice.

Poems from *Teasing Roots from the Stem of a Geranium* – the collection that won the Patrick Kavanagh Poetry Award – had previously won the Clogh Writers' Poetry Award in 1999 and the Poetry on the Wall Competition (run by South Dublin Libraries) in 2000. Commended in the British National Poetry Awards in 1999, she has been a runner-up in several other UK competitions, including that of *Stand Magazine*. In 2000 she won a prize in the UK New Writer Award, the Gerard Manley Hopkins Award and the Maria Edgeworth Award. Her poems have been broadcast on Irish radio and published in Irish, UK and German journals. Some have also been translated into Russian and Dutch.

Mince Customer

Pinned to the door
was a diagram of a heifer
with sections straight-lined

across her side: sirloin
jigsawed between rib
and rump, shank slotting

into round. And the people
who came in, we sorted them
by the cuts they bought:

Mince customers wanted cosseting,
all the work done for them;
A fillet woman wanted only lean,

leaving all the fat
and gristle on our hands;
But a brisket man

was a prince, who'd take
his lean where he could get it
between the bone and thews.

Inside too a series of lines
ran through the house like skewers.
As a child you couldn't see them,

but bit by bit you'd puzzle out
the no-nonsense pattern they laid down,
plot yourself a course in which

your silverside was out
with your flank protected
your tenderloin concealed

or else you'd feel the chill
from the refrigeration unit
as sure as any mince customer.

Sorcerer

for my mother

Jam jars baking in the oven
Bolsters boiling for apple jelly
Bread poultice to draw a splinter
Butter paper to line a loaf tin
Fish cakes for a Friday
'Halibut Orange' to curb the winter

She'd goad a ground-down tin-opener into cutting
Scoop a daddy-long-legs up in her fingers
Prise a tight-lipped lid from a jar of jam
Soft soap the twin-tub into jiggling and chuckling
Pluck the harm from a phrase over dinner
Tease roots from the stem of a geranium

We thought alchemy was something you took
with tea, that magic was made from cookbooks.

Cold Storage

There was a cold room
at the back of our house.

Our father propped the door open,
and the butcher shouldered sides of beef,
and sheep slit down their spines.

Speared on hooks they hung,
flanked by ox-tongues, long and thick
as a healthy man's thigh.

On the floor lay fleshy chickens
packed in boxes, their hearts and sweating
entrails bagged within their breasts.

Upstairs, you and I peered at the silver
fleck on a fish's eye in the kitchen
foreground of a painting by Velasquez,

or turned the page to trace the head
of John the Baptist through strips of greaseproof
meant to parcel out rack chops and T-bone steaks.

Later, after you and I had gone, our mother
scrubbed splatters of blood from the concrete,
hoovered up the last flake of sawdust.

The room – windowless and airless
but no longer cold – stood empty but for
wool coats and leather jackets

that assembled there and hung
side-by-side like distant cousins
of the earlier occupants.

Now it's my turn to stand with my back
against the door, as the removal
men deliver boxes crammed

with kitchen knives, a fold-up barbecue,
your College thesis, Labour Party card,
out-sized atlas, home-made chess pieces.

Still wrapped in tissue, they lie on the floor,
in the dark, waiting … to be sectioned up
portioned out, bartered with siblings

each one trying to piece the present
back together bit by bit; each one after
the thing that seems to have your heart in it.

A House Divided

I'm applying paper to the window-panes
pouring boiling water down the outflow pipes
sealing off the air vents with Vaseline
muzzling the letter-box with masking tape;
I've given up feeling bad about men.

I've plastered putty round the back door frame
ditched the doormat in the hawthorn hedge
filled a skip with high heels, flimsy underwear
buried cut stems in the sweet pea bed;
I can't see any further use for them.

I won't unhook the security chain
when my groceries come from Tesco.
I'll slip the boy a tip and wait for him
to go before I open back the door;
No one will ever get to me again.

Once my e-mail's disconnected, I'll turn on
the PC – not living I'll want to write about it,
not feeling I'll find myself imagining
it, my effusions saved to floppy disc;
I'll never be in need of anything.

Feelings I'll then confine to drawers, not loose
in the house careering up the gable
walls like cracks. But sorted as to source,
labelled 'good', 'bad' or 'grey & intangible'.
I'm hoping for lots of the latter; of course,
I've given up feeling.

A Good Rogeting

I keep to myself on one side of a bed
whose other half is occupied by books
meant to match my moods, catch the thread
of all my thoughts, from hard-angled works
of reference, to magazines, loose-leaf pads.
A collection of love-lorn verse
hugs an impenetrable masterpiece
while Judith Hearne's eclipsed by glamour ads.

When I bring a new one back
over dinner with a glass of wine
I imagine removing its paper bag
running my fingers down its spine
how I'll fan the pages to inhale
its pristine smell, then make it my own:
easing back the sleeve and going down
on the biographical detail.

Sometimes that's the best bit
on evenings when I'm not in form
to get stuck in or to commit
not even to paper. One volume
alone then seems able to interject:
Chambers Twentieth Century Dictionary –
something new with every read
and no long-term effects.

I can fall asleep over a phrase whose
meaning remains a stranger and wake
in the morning with *Roget's Thesaurus*
poking me urgently in the back.

2002

Alice Lyons, a poet and painter, was born in 1960 in
Paterson, New Jersey, to first- and second-generation Irish
emigrants. She grew up in the United States and was
educated at Connecticut College, the University of
Pennsylvania and Boston University. She has taught English
and painting at Boston University and Maine College of Art.
Since 1998 she has made her home in Cootehall, Co.
Roscommon.

Her poems have appeared in numerous journals in the US,
UK and Ireland, including *Barrow Street*, Mermaid
Turbulence's *Element*, *Margie: The American Journal of
Poetry*, *Poetry Ireland Review*, *The SHOp* and *Modern
Painters*. Her paintings are in the collections of University
College Galway and the Office of Public Works and she
currently lectures in painting at GMIT Galway and Castlebar.
She has received a Bursary in Literature from the Arts
Council of Ireland, an award from the Academy of American
Poets and, recently, an Ireland Chair of Poetry Trust Bursary.

Alice Lyons has just completed her first collection of poems,
speck, the earlier version of which received the Patrick
Kavanagh Poetry Award.

Unfinished Painting

for John Walker and Anne Harris

It will not be square.

It will convince you to keep going.

It will be made with Williamsburg
Nickel yellow, a direct hit
To the nervous system.

It will certainly disturb
Yes, it will unhinge.

It will sound like a gong clanging
Like a mute guest at a cocktail party.

It will enfold you in your
'We regret to inform you' moments.

Its History will make you feel like a speck.

You will fear you might slash it.

The skin of its surface
Will make you ache.
Your streetclothes will boil
With flicking tongues
Will billow with hot breath.
Your breasts might leak milk.

It will be lit
With a silvery light
Its lead white ground will incandesce.

Its darkness will threaten to swallow
You will suffer an attack
Of vertigo in the void
An elevator drop in the gut.

You will grope for something solid.
You will be told it is dead.
You will convince yourself it is dead.
You will turn it to face the wall.

It will bleed through the other side.
Pools of blood will form on your floor.
The blood will rise until
All your windows are scarlet.

You will try to staunch this wound.
You cannot make such a tourniquet.

This painting is worth nothing.
You will dash into an inferno for it.

It will be varnished with the tears
Shed on your birthing bed.

Paintings of Martyrs Speak
National Museum of Catalan Art, Barcelona

God forgive her for laughing
At my un-comic dilemma.
I am sliced from my noggin
To my solar plexus
By an enormous (and sharp)
Urine-yellow saw.
My wound is a zig-zag of blood –
She thinks it's a funny zipper.
Many prayers were distracted
In that Pyreneean chapel
By me, I hope to God by me
And not my serrated foe.
I am a gory fiasco
And she is in stitches.

Same with us twins in the cauldron.
We've made our medieval eyes to plead.
See the beady-eyed devil stoking the fire?
See others scuttling at some evil preparation?
We are doomed for pagan soup
And she's marvelling at viridian intervals
Between my devout sibling and me.

We were put here on this fresco
To instruct, to strike fear.
What's become of our world
When people see past us
As in a two-way mirror?
Sliced and boiled for the mystery
Of faith and transubstantiation
Now it is we who are unseen.

The Polish Language
for Barbara Falkowska and her family

If language could shrug shoulders
lift eyebrows and turn palms up
you might have a tiny idea.

To make an effigy, you'd need
a lot of concrete, more than you'd think
a stork, some amber
honey from bees that live near rape
a quantity of shirts freely removed
from the backs of anyone you meet
big lumps of lead and coal
and a great deal of wood from a primeval forest.

A poultice of sliced onions on the throat
may help you speak it.

Cats are known to rub up against its sibilance.

Crush a cherry and a beet
in your fingers to arrive at its colour –
czerwony.
If that fails to convince, make a soup.

When you are fed up with the world
say *sprzykrzy*
or phone information in Zakopane
and just listen.

As a matter of fact
in this sonorous, consonant tongue
my art was revivified.

My Polish brothers and sisters
in art (the ones who survived)
robbed of flint you made fire
out of evil you wrote *live*.

Thank God It's Dry

Disregarding Mary in the post office
the Mary with the permanent hairnet:
It's promised bad. She headed off
any brazen praise of bold good
weather. Six years coming this
heat wave over Ireland. Mesmeric
the buzzing bees, checking stalks
of self-heal the way you'd check for mail

in the 'pigeon hole' before e-mail.
The lost years. How real life stalks
the meat of you. Mesmeric
the cabbage white – bouncing dot in this
karaoke meadow. It sings a song of good
death. You lifted his coffin and headed off
for Mass behind a cousin in sleazy fishnets
the weight on four shoulders and off his.

2003

Manus McManus was born in Dublin in 1959. He
lived in the USA for nine years and began writing poetry
after his return to Ireland in 1994.

He was awarded third prize in the Strokestown Poetry
Competition in 1999 and was short-listed for the Seacat Irish
National Poetry Competition in 2002. His poems have
appeared in *The Irish Times* and *Poetry Ireland*. He works
in the Irish Film Archive.

Story

We arrive
without introduction, though
there may be notes at the end.
I don't know
what to say about the radiance
we become blind to, or how
bones grow from spilled milk,
or the wisdom that guides us
to the people from whom
we will be snatched away.
I can't say
if I shall remember the tiger
who smiles in my words
as they tear at your clothes,
or these summer nights
that will drag us into winter.
I can't tell you
who we really are, though death
will not mistake us.
I'm trying
not to think about clay, or stones
sinking down through clay,
splitting damp hermetic wood.
Looking into our graves,
we see no way home.
Our hope
implies things: the handle
on the door is a candle that we lit
twenty years before. And yet it is
dark down there. A lighthouse beam
would travel half an inch
through what they call 'loam'.

Waking in Pennsylvania,
Near the Irish Sea

The cold current slips by the breast of the eider duck; the bells
ring out on the shoal; ships stand off in the mist.

Waking from home, I turn from you in silence. I no longer
speak my nostalgia. What swims up from the deep is always
the wrong word.

Home: faintly now I hear the surf, and lie beside you,
where your white back gleams in a fold of the waves. Again
I am living uncertainly.

***

On the face of the clock a luminous constellation swings into
the east: a quarter past three, Sunday morning. Down in the
deep, no red-letter days, but the steady rotting of ships and
their cargos. Rolling skulls and soup tins. Featherweed
crossing the cabin-lights. Red velvet curtains.

On our wedding day our words sank in, an irretrievable
weight. Are they the treasure we must dive for, again
and again?

***

Of our love, I wonder if you remember: my grief-stricken
Byzantine faces, eyes open like drowned men as I came.

The Remote Loves of Men

1

They are not neighbourly. They disdain what fails to make them
overflow. They will always bear the ignominy of a random
destination.

'Plato would have you recycled as wolves!'

What I was thinking, just after you opened your blouse, was
how much I am pining for my reticence.

2

The wild ones, they bound away through the snow into the
woods. Their teeth leave a trail of tears all the way to the kill.
Which of them, fighting for his portion, will bite his tongue?

3

If you tame one: in the beginning you look over your shoulder to
see if he is still behind you. His spirit follows you everywhere,
with a slight limp. He will feed from your hand.

In later years, you'll give him what you have to spare. But
then – when he is slow, and sleeps long, and moths mistake
him for an old coat and those yellow eyes follow you around
as if you were his mother – the secret fear that he might revert
will be, for you, the only pleasure. What he can hope for is to
die utterly. Then to be dust.

4

I am not unusual, in that I have always harboured a secret wish
to be everywhere. On the old planet, at the edge of the desert,
on the cliffs beneath the ocean, shepherds would track me in the
night sky.

Houses of Cape May

Trying to write a poem of explanation –
Perhaps there are children in me
only as there are sonnets
in the squid's dark inkwells –
I grow tired of having left you,

and go to haunt the window.
Crossing the mullion now,
high up in the sky, a jet leaves
a vapour trail on its journey west;
there are people waiting inside that too,

moving down the map from Ireland,
over the whale-blue canyons,
of the mid-Atlantic rift
to the Gulf of St Lawrence,
Boston, New York, Cape May,
dropping toward summer.

My love is up in the air
above the old landing place.
That neighbourhood
where we might have lived:
I have been there, at night,
swimming in the water towers.

At Rickett's Glen

for Richard Vargo

We wander the dark spruce above the lake,
return to camp through wood smoke
under October trees, falling leaves
the lamps of Palestine going out along the shore.

We do not remember the history of our cells,
or where the lost tribes have gone:
when we drink by the campfire
the autumn air is happy in our lungs.

Surely we must carry some good in our veins,
though what is past and what is to come
are unconsoled by our words. Orion climbs
the branches and flies up from the trees.

Inside each bottle a bubbling planetarium
brings us closer to our lives. 'In the deepest
water', says Tu Fu, 'is the fish's utmost joy.'
The midnight wind races over the lake.

In the morning we cannot find the storm lamp
and silently blame our neighbours.
The car brooks no less than seventy
on the highway back to town.

The rain comes down. Pine trees
graze the horizon of our old retreat;
as we pass them they drift away
on the stubble of the cornfields.

What is our refuge to be when we
get back to our homes?
If only we could believe in the soul,
a strange hero like a shaman

flying through the walls of asylums,
and remember how we came here,
in the plum-coloured raindrops
on the hull of your car.

* 'In the deepest water is the fish's utmost joy' comes from 'The Autumn Wastes'
  by the T'ang poet, Tu Fu (trans. A.C. Graham).

It Is Not Often that I Write

I see in you the gift of a lost home,
the pain that is generous to everything I write.
I think of the elm outside our old room:
high branches waving in the night
where squirrels gather blue moons.